For chef Ashley Christensen, the diner is a metaphor for comfort, inclusivity, and extremely good food. Poole's Diner, with its signature double-horseshoe bar, is a life force, breathing energy into what was a languishing downtown, giving a new voice and relevance to Southern food, and catalyzing a community around eating together. The story of Poole's is emblematic of its visionary chef. It celebrates what is humble and good, and shares what is personal and special to her so it can become personal and special to others. And who wouldn't want to partake of *Malted Slaw*, *Royale with Cheese*, *Pork and Dumplings with Stewed Tomatoes and Butter Beans*, and *Strawberry Shortcakes with Rhubarb Marmalade*. Anchored by a dozen go-to techniques for the best cornbread, foolproof vinaigrettes, and roasted tomatoes that enhance any dish, *Poole's* is both a document of the place and a roadmap to eating, cooking, and living with compassion and exuberance.

Poole's

recipes and stories
from a modern diner

ASHLEY CHRISTENSEN

with Kaitlyn Goalen

photography by Johnny Autry

TEN SPEED PRESS
Berkeley

Recipe Contents VI

For Eliza

Recipe Contents

Welcome.

Diners are an American fixture. They're a piece of every town, and usually they're not much to look at: worn countertops, free refills on coffee, an everyman's clientele. Typically the genre doesn't offer much in the way of memorable cuisine, but it delivers a sense of dependability. It seems like everybody I know has a soft spot for some diner, somewhere. Perhaps it provided refuge on a late-night road trip, or it has the only breakfast that will cure your hangover. Maybe it's the place you went on Sundays with your grandparents. As one of the most accessible forms of restaurant, diners are places where strangers can find familiarity through food, whether it's meatloaf and mashed potatoes, a straightforward burger, or chicken potpie.

This is the story of one such diner and of the people and food that belong to it.

Introduction

AN INTRODUCTION (AND REINTRODUCTION) TO POOLE'S DINER.

I first stepped inside Poole's Diner when I was about eighteen. I had just moved to Raleigh for college and was drawn to the small shotgun space, then called the Vertigo Diner, because several of my older friends worked there and would let me drink a few beers without asking for ID. During an era in Raleigh in which the downtown area had little nightlife, the Vertigo, and one adjacent music venue, were anchors that drew in a young, creative class of students and musicians along with a beloved cast of bar regulars.

Despite its neon-green walls and plentiful use of tchotchkes to cover nearly every free surface, I felt an immediate kinship with the place. The geometry of the double-horseshoe bar induced easy conversation with your neighbor, and the room seemed to magnify the energy of its patrons. I ended up working there, first as a bartender and then in the kitchen as part of the weekend brunch crew. It was one of my first jobs in a real restaurant kitchen. After a few months, the owners put me in charge of the shift, and I created my first menu.

Each Sunday I would show up for work and the hours would speed by as we figured out how to serve a meal from a tiny kitchen with outdated equipment. I was still in school, toying with the idea that I wanted to go into the music industry, and hadn't admitted to myself that cooking was my true path. But I loved it: the work, the people, the hustle.

After about eighteen months, I moved onto a new job at a nearby restaurant called the Humble Pie. Leaving the Vertigo, I couldn't have imagined that it was just the first act of a multipart story, and that I'd be returning to my beginnings in more ways than one.

Shortly into my tenure at Humble Pie, my father was in town visiting from New York. He ate in the restaurant during our first New Year's Eve service, and after we'd finished, he suggested that we visit "that Vertigo place you're always talking about" for a drink. We drove the handful of blocks over to McDowell Street, and when we got out of the car, he looked like he'd seen a ghost. "This isn't the Vertigo," he said. "This is Poole's Luncheonette, and I used to eat lunch here every day when I lived in Raleigh." He looked across the road, reeling with the

I had no idea what shape my menu would take or exactly how the room would look. I just knew how I wanted to make people feel.

weight of the memory. "And that building on the corner. That was the building I was drafted out of in 1967." We drank our drinks with goose-bumps as he recalled what he remembered of the menu back then, thoroughly awestruck that history had rolled back on itself.

The Vertigo Diner, it turns out, was just a recent incarnation of one of the oldest restaurants in the city, originally called Poole's. When it first opened in 1945, it was Poole's Pie Shop; the owners later expanded the menu and rechristened it Poole's Luncheonette. Then for years, it was called Poole's Diner. In the 1990s, the daughter (and her husband) of the original proprietor, John Poole, decided to get out of the restaurant business and leased the building to new tenants, who gave it a new identity as the Vertigo.

I wouldn't cross paths with the space again for another seven or eight years. With a handful of cooking jobs under my belt, I was itching to start my own project and put the word out that I was looking for a space. Within three days, Susan, the owner of the Vertigo (which, incidentally, had been renamed Poole's again), was looking to sell her lease. I met her to look at the space, and even through the neon green on the walls and the dusty tchotchkes, I knew that I wanted it. I had no idea what shape my menu would take or exactly how the room would look. I just knew how I wanted to make people feel, and it was clear to me that I could achieve it in that space. I called my parents after the walk-through and told them my plans. "This is the smartest thing you've ever done," they said. And within a few days, I'd made a full-price offer on Poole's Diner.

Anyone who has opened a restaurant will tell you that the process *never* goes according to plan. I purchased the lease as part of a "turn-key" deal, meaning that I inherited all of the kitchen equipment and supplies. I figured it would take about a month of deep cleaning and a new coat of paint to get up and running, so I went ahead and hired a sous chef, Sunny Gerhart, to help things move along more quickly.

Then, three days after I took possession of the building, the one-hundred-gallon water heater in the kitchen died. (A blessing in disguise, but it was the first sign that my timeline might have been a bit off.) And on deeper examination, the ancient hood, suspended by chains over the stove, also needed replacing. The closer we looked, the more we realized that we were in for a more taxing refurbishment than we thought. All in all, between permitting with the city and getting new equipment, it took us about a year to get the place in shape. I was beyond broke, working half a job as a consulting chef and paying two full salaries, in addition to the insurmountable bills that piled up from the unforeseen construction expenses. We borrowed more money and kept going.

Poole's Pie Shop – Dec. 1956

Down[town]
after its pool of c[ustomers]

BY STEVEN EISENSTADT
STAFF WRITER

RALEIGH — Yet another downtown Raleigh institution disappeared Friday when Poole's Luncheonette fried up its last cheeseburgers, chicken platters and country ham sandwiches.

Fittingly, the 47-year-old diner closed early on its final day for lack of customers.

The South McDowell Street restaurant had been losing money for several years as its bread and butter — nearby businesses that supplied a pool of hungry workers — closed or moved to the suburbs, manager Bill Hicks said.

For a time, Poole's owner was able to stick it out with loyal

patronage ...
tele ran...
yuppies ...
things ...

The ...
Mot...
m...
d...

o...
tran...
Raleigh. ...
cent Parrish-H...
a site near Raleigh-...
national Airport.

Add to those departures...
impending relocations of th...
other downtown landmarks — Sir
Walter Chevrolet, Briggs Hard-

... meal

...iving
...e just

...her blow
..., decided
... owned by
... late father,
...t. But it was
... place.
...truth, I'm ready
...aid between ciga-
...burgers sizzled on
...ehind him. "I'm just
...alk out the door the
... I came in: without a

SEE **DINER**, PAGE 3B

SANDWICHES

...for good, Manager Bill Hicks
...mers linger over their meals.

LUNCHEO[N]

TODAY   SAT. Nov. 24, 1994   News + Observer

the guest: At Poole's, the use of the word *customer* (the "c" word) is strictly forbidden. Say it, and you'll inevitably get called out with withering looks. We proudly use the word *guest*. I am a firm believer that to recognize the people who eat with us as simply customers cheapens the experience we create together. It implies a transaction, a simple exchange of tender for goods. But dining out should be more than a transaction; it's a relationship. We're a part of our guests' day, and they are a part of what drives us to push for greatness. Food and drink play a role, but in respect and appreciation of community, there is so much more to it. It takes what we do from making a meal, to making a commitment to our life's work. Is the customer always right? Who can say. Most importantly at Poole's, the guest is always welcome.

Finally, on December 13, 2007, we opened for business. We had finished the menu two days prior, just after getting our final permits. To say the opening crew was lean would be an understatement: we had one bartender, two servers, no host, and just me, Sunny, and one poor guy, Justin, who had never worked in a restaurant before, in the kitchen. Somehow, word had gotten around that we were open, and the place was just packed out the gate. All of a sudden, the ticket line was a sea of handwritten paper tickets. I remember peering out into the dining room and just thinking, "Oh wow." Because there was no host, crowds of people were standing between the tables, waiting for folks to get up. People had no idea what to do with the chalkboard menus and kept asking for menus. It was chaos, and I'm pretty sure the food took about two hours to come out that night.

Luckily, we figured it out pretty quickly. We staffed up. We bought more glassware. We cried a few times. Then one Saturday night, things synced up and we crushed that service. It started to feel real. For the first few months, we had no prep cooks, so Sunny and I would show up every morning at 7:00 a.m. to start our prep. We'd finish cleaning up the kitchen after dinner service just in time to catch last call at our own bar, and then we would stay up making the next set of menus until about 3:00 a.m., before doing it all again the next day. It was during those late-night planning sessions, when the restaurant was dark and we were more exhausted than we'd ever been in our lives, that we'd turn to each other, giddy like kids, with barely enough energy to raise our beers, and I'd say, "I can't believe we're doing this, I can't believe I own a restaurant." There was so much pride. Nothing could have prepared me for that feeling.

That first year, there were so many lessons (well, let's be honest, there are still so many lessons). We slowly improved and optimized how we would run each shift, tweaking and honing it to deliver that feeling I'd set out to create for people: comfort. And as we passed through the seasons of our first year, the menu found its footing. Some dishes were obvious from the very beginning, while others came more slowly, as we responded to the natural evolution of what the place had become. At the heart of the menu, though, I drew from my own sources of comfort—the food I grew up on—as the inspiration for what we were doing.

New, vital members joined the team, people like Matt Fern, who started as a bartender and ended up as the general manager of Poole's for years and as one of my best friends on the planet. For so many of our guests, Poole's is synonymous with him. Some of our team departed and went on to new adventures. Some departed, and ultimately came back. We developed regulars, people who came on such a frequent basis as to feel a sense of ownership in this place. In using the original name, Poole's Diner, I knew that I was tapping into a collective memory, a fixture that could continue to act as an anchor for a city that was changing and evolving. Without even realizing it, opening Poole's Diner turned me into a community organizer.

GIVE UNTIL IT HURTS.

The fairy godmother behind the scenes of the Poole's origin story is Eliza Kraft Olander. I first met Eliza when I was working at Enoteca Vin, where she was a regular. By the time that I met her, she was a full-time philanthropist, serving on the boards of multiple nonprofits and raising hundreds of thousands of dollars each year for charitable causes. But she is also a veteran of the restaurant industry. She went from owning a single Burger King franchise to running a company that controlled many of the Burger King and Applebee's locations in three states. Unfailingly generous, she quickly took me into her circle and was the first person to show me the huge impact that I could have as a chef simply by being present, championing a cause, and cooking some food.

When the time came to purchase Poole's, Eliza fronted me the money. And when we needed more money, she came in as a partner, helping us make it through the unexpected bumps in the road in order to get the doors open without sacrificing our principles. Knowing how difficult the industry was, she told me not to worry about beginning to pay back our loan until our thirty-sixth month of operation, an incredibly generous display of trust and a relief to me, a first-time business owner. She gave us room to figure out what we were doing, and to do it well. It turns out, though, that we didn't need the grace period: by month thirty-five, she was paid back in full. (Needless to say, she was impressed.)

For Eliza, supporting Poole's was about more than helping out a friend. She saw, even before I did, the potential of that restaurant to help catalyze a desolate downtown. For her, the act of cooking for others has a sort of power, even a responsibility. And in helping me recognize that, she inspired me to turn a modest diner into a platform for giving back. Since we first met, we've teamed up on numerous events, fund-raisers, boards, and charities. Together we've raised millions. Literally. It hasn't always been easy, but Eliza has a saying that I'm fond of repeating when I'm feeling tired or grumpy: "Give until it hurts."

Without even realizing it, opening Poole's Diner turned me into a community organizer.

ps —

vinaigrettes

dess

☆ROA...
HERB-SCENTED

VER PATE WITH $9
...ER & PEACH MOSTARDA

☆BIBB LETTUCE WITH $8
VACCHE ROSSO PARMIGIANO REGGIANO
& RED WINE VINAIGRETTE

☆ROASTED...
OAT CRISPS & C...

☆ CRAB BEIGNETS WI...
HEIRLOOM TOMATOES, MARI...
& MALT AIOLI

...HEESE WITH $9
...R CHEDDAR & CROSTINI

☆ROASTED BEETS WITH $12
GRILLED PEACH, BURRATA,
& BLACKBERRY VINAIGRETTE

☆ PEACH & BLUEBERRY COBBLER
WITH SOUR CREAM ICE CREAM

☆ PAN-SEARED KING...
SUMMER SQUASH, BASIL, SP...
ROASTED TOMATO

...IN TUNA WITH $14
...NI, MARINATED PEPPERS,
...CADO

☆HEIRLOOM TOMATOES WITH $12
GRILLED CORNBREAD, CELERY,
& BUTTERMILK BLUE

☆ VIDERI DARK CHOCOLATE
PUDDING WITH JACKED UP OLIVE OIL CAKE

☆PORK & DUMPLINGS WITH...
RICOTTA GNOCCHI, STEWED...

SWEET CORN SOUP WITH $10
...OMATOES & CORN RELISH

☆LOCAL WATERMELON WITH $13
GOAT LADY DAIRY CHEVRE, AVOCADO, BASIL,
& VIDALIA ONION VINAIGRETTE

☆10 OZ ROYALE WITH CARR...
GRILLED BRIOCHE, & RED...

☆AN 18% GRATUITY MAY BE ADDED TO PARTIES OF 6 OR MORE
☆ CONSUMING RAW OR UNDERCOOKED MEAT, POULTRY, SEAFOOD, OR
EGGS MAY INCREASE YOUR RISK OF FOODBORNE ILLNESS
☆TO RECEIVE EMAILS ABOUT UPCOMING EVENTS, PLEASE
SIGN UP FOR OUR MAILING LIST AT THE HOST STAND

FINDING THE COMFORT IN COMFORT FOOD.

I never went to culinary school, but I struggle with the phrase "self-taught chef." I was raised in a family that loves food, and my learning started early.

My father, Fox, was a truck driver while I was growing up, and on his trips he became obsessed with studying the dives and diners that defined each city he visited. He smuggled home recipes by way of his memory, and upon his return, would re-create his findings for us: New Orleans's red beans and rice, or Cincinnati chili over fat spaghetti noodles. Food was about the place it came from, and Fox loved to take us to all of the places he'd been, one spoonful at a time.

In his time off of the road, he gardened with a nearly competitive, survivalist energy. Long before words like *organic* hit the mainstream,

POOLE'S

he was making pesticides out of dead-bug carcasses for his two huge gardens. He would dry summer herbs on the dashboard of his Volvo, taking care to park it with the windshield positioned perfectly to grab the midday sunshine. He crossed the neighbor's tobacco field to visit his hive of bees and to harvest the honey that would be the only idea of *sugar* my brother, Zak, and I would know though our early childhood.

My mother, Lynn, was no less fervent about her love of food. An army brat who grew up in England, Japan, and Memphis, her time abroad seemed to have instilled in her a deepened appreciation for the idea of what we'd now call "local" eating. To her, Southern food was defined by what grew in the Southern earth.

In Kernersville, North Carolina, where I grew up, Fox and Lynn made a life of gardening, cooking, imbibing, and entertaining. Dinner was never a rote exercise; it was an occasion, an experience. Unlike the structured schedules of some of my schoolmates who sat down to eat their meal at the same time each night, dinnertime was unpredictable at my house. We ate when it was ready, which meant after my parents had enjoyed winding down the day with a glass of wine and some tunes, while cooking a meal that was as much about the process as the finished product. Often, we ate as late as 9:00 p.m. (on a school night, no less).

My parents often danced as they cooked, slightly buzzed and in love with the moment. It would embarrass me, because I was young and shy. But I also secretly knew it was special. They loved our life, they loved each other, and they loved us. In that kitchen, where they cooked and danced, my emotional education in food was born.

When I'd started working in professional kitchens, I tried to make up for my lack of formal training by soaking up as much information as I could. Having never lived outside of North Carolina, I read cookbooks voraciously to learn about other regional cuisines, and I often worked two jobs at once so I could get more exposure to different styles and methods. At one point, while I was working as a caterer, I started pulling a few shifts at Enoteca Vin, the restaurant where I first met Eliza Kraft Olander. The place had one of the most ambitious and contemporary wine lists in the state at the time, and the chef, a woman named Andrea Reusing, was bringing in local ingredients that nobody in the city had access to before. I worked there on barter; instead of collecting a paycheck, I'd bank my earnings and put them toward coming in on my nights off and eating and drinking at the bar, teaching myself about wine and how the plates we created in the kitchen felt in the context of the dining room. (Ultimately, Andrea left to open a restaurant called Lantern in nearby Chapel Hill, and about a year later, I took over the chef role at Vin, which I held until I opened Poole's.)

When it came time to design the menu at Poole's, I started with a feeling. I remembered the way it felt to eat dinner as a kid with my parents—it was an escape from the day, but also a reminder of its bless-ings. It was a process, a gathering space, a warmth. And I funneled that style of cooking through the context of all that I'd learned from other chefs and mentors; I translated it into the language of local ingredients and molded it to pay homage to the diner roots of our space.

The result was Macaroni au Gratin, Roast Chicken, Luck and Money, Bibb Lettuce Salad with Red Wine Vinaigrette, and all of the other recipes that you'll find in these pages. And I'll be honest: in the begin-ning it felt like a gamble. In a time when food was becoming increasingly important and chefs in big cities were pushing all kinds of boundaries, I had to suppress the kernel of self-doubt that what I was doing wasn't sophisticated enough. Compared to the temples of fine dining that were making headlines in New York and San Francisco, this food, my food, looked more akin to a category of cooking that many were labeling as low-brow: comfort food. I anxiously persevered, choosing to cook the dishes that felt true to me, a kid who grew up in the sticks of North Carolina. I knew that anything else would feel like an ill-fitting costume and fall short of producing the kind of experience I'd set out to create.

So instead of distinguishing our menu with theatrics or reinventing the wheel, we focused on the subtleties of every ingredient and every technique, pushing ourselves to balance flavor within the familiarity of dishes that everyone knew and loved.

Almost a decade later, as I see more and more chefs go back to the basics and celebrate what is close and precious, I feel so grateful for the confluence of people and events that enabled me to find my voice and use Poole's as my pulpit. Since we opened, Raleigh has changed in almost unrecognizable ways: downtown is flourishing with new businesses, and a new workforce of craftsmen and creators has risen up. We have opened new restaurants (six and counting), each with its own special vibe and amazing team, each a part of what is now a rather large family.

We have used our food as a lightening rod for building a community, for supporting one another and others, for making our city the only place we could ever imagine calling home. My greatest hope for this book is that these recipes can inspire you to do the same.

Using this book

The distance between the restaurant version and the home cook version of my food is probably smaller than it is for most chefs. Our dishes are familiar and straightforward. If you order something called "deviled egg," you'll get a deviled egg. No smoke, no mirrors.

So how are these recipes different? What makes them stand apart?

For each and every dish, we start by breaking it down, piece by piece, and examining it, from the ingredients on up through every single step. We pay meticulous attention to the details to make sure everything is in balance and the final product is absolutely delicious while still respecting its identity and origin story. One of the most important parts of this process is in seasoning.

For me, seasoning is a much greater consideration than whether or not something needs a sprinkle of salt or a few cracks of pepper. It also includes acidity, richness, sharpness, and heat. Here is a breakdown of the various techniques and ingredients we use to season our food. You'll see them revisited throughout the course of the recipes that follow.

Salt

My go-to seasoning is fine (as in fine textured, not fancy-fine) sea salt. La Baleine sel fin is what you'll find next to every station in the Poole's kitchen. Note that sea salt is saltier than kosher.

When seasoning the surface of an ingredient I'm about to char, whether a steak or a vegetable, I hold the salt canister at eye level (more than two feet above the surface) and salt from that distance. It creates a more even layer of salt than seasoning from just a few inches above, which has an uneven, zigzag effect. If I'm making a brine or a cure (see right) or seasoning pasta water, I use kosher salt.

Pepper

Most of the recipes in this book call for a certain number of cranks of the pepper mill instead of a specific measurement of black pepper. This is because there is a huge, huge flavor chasm between freshly ground black pepper and the ground pepper that you buy in a canister in the spice aisle of the supermarket. It might seem like a small thing, but I just can't overstate how much of an effect freshly ground pepper has on your food. A gorgeous seared-off rib eye just isn't the same without it—and why on earth, when you've purchased a pricey steak to make for dinner, would you mistreat it with dried-out, dusty preground pepper?

I prefer old-school pepper grinders that you actually crank the top of—the kind your waiter pulls out tableside to season your Caesar salad. For general seasoning, I keep the grind at a medium level—not too coarse, not too fine.

When I refer to "cranks" in the recipes in this book, I mean a single 180-degree turn of the grinder. Four cranks equal about ⅛ teaspoon of freshly ground black pepper.

Toasting Peppercorns

There are two recipes in this book, both of them signature dishes at Poole's, where pepper isn't just a seasoning, it's a full-blown star ingredient: Pimento Cheese (page 33) and Royale with Cheese (page 209). Both recipes call for finely ground toasted peppercorns. You could, of course, use regular pepper out of your pepper mill—there won't be any serious repercussions. But for the sake of comparison, I urge you to try giving your peppercorns a toast (in a dry skillet over high heat for about 90 seconds) before grinding. It makes the flavor of the pepper significantly more robust and fiery. Grind the pepper finely, and sift it through a fine-mesh sieve to create an even texture. Toasted, finely ground pepper will keep in a lidded container in your pantry for up to 1 month before the flavors begin to dull. Toasting is also a technique I like to employ with chile flakes. Place the chile flakes in a dry skillet and toast over high heat for 90 seconds. It activates the oils in the pepper, which enhances the flavor.

Brines and Cures

I am a devout follower of the church of brines. I know there are plenty of finicky cheffy prep steps out there in the world—mostly things that just seem to add time to the cooking process while hardly moving the needle on flavor. *Brining is not one of those.* In fact, it's just the opposite: simple as breathing and with a huge flavor payoff.

Most cookbooks talk about brines in relation to chicken and turkey, but really that's just the tip of the iceberg. In this book, you'll find ice brines for salmon and shrimp, as well as seasoned shock water for blanched vegetables (thanks to Steven Satterfield for schooling me on the salted shock water). I even brine cabbage before making slaw. Brining is the simplest thing you can do to season an ingredient to its core. It works best on dense ingredients like proteins, but it can also work to great effect with dense vegetables like broccoli (and cabbage).

Here are some quick brine formulas.

FOR ONE 3- TO 4-POUND WHOLE CHICKEN

Mix 4 cups room-temperature water with 6 tablespoons kosher salt and 3 tablespoons sugar until dissolved. Stir in 4 cups ice-cold water. Submerge the chicken for 12 hours, then drain and pat dry with paper towels.

FOR 1 POUND FISH OR SHRIMP

Mix 2 cups water and ½ cup kosher salt until combined. Stir in 4 cups ice water. Submerge the fish for 20 minutes, then drain and pat dry with paper towels.

VEGETABLES

Any time you blanch hearty vegetables such as broccoli or brussels sprouts in salted water, consider adding salt to your ice bath too, as it will help the vegetables retain that seasoning while stopping the cooking.

For a salted ice water bath (ice brine): Mix 8 cups water with ¼ cup kosher salt until the salt dissolves. Add 8 cups ice. Drain the blanched vegetables and submerge them in the salted ice water for 1 minute before draining again and spinning dry in a salad spinner.

When working with brines, make sure you dry your ingredients well after brining. For proteins, just pat down with paper towels; for vegetables, I use a salad spinner to remove as much excess water as possible. Then I'll set the vegetables in a colander over the sink until I need them.

PICKLE BRINE

If you live in the South, you can almost take pickles for granted. My pantry is always full of jars of pickles, a mix of unidentified versions received as gifts and those I've put up or purchased at the farmers' market (we're lucky to have a pretty incredible local preservationist, April McGreger of Farmer's Daughter, who sells the most amazing pickles you've ever had at the farmers' market in nearby Durham).

Having a stock of pickles on hand is a great, fast way to build depth and flavor in a dish without a tremendous amount of effort. Chop the pickles and coat with herbs and olive oil for a quick relish, add them to a salad as an addition to fresh vegetables, or serve them alongside Chicken Liver Mousse (page 41) or Duck Rillettes (page 39).

Here are my two workhorse brines, one suited to winter vegetables like beets, carrots, pumpkin (yes, pumpkin!), or onions, and the other perfect for summer harvests, including cucumbers, peppers, okra, green tomatoes, or string beans.

Winter Pickle Brine

6 cups cider vinegar

4 cups sugar

½ cup kosher salt

1½-inch piece ginger, peeled and sliced into coins

¼ cup black peppercorns

8 whole cloves

2 star anise pods

In a large saucepot over high heat, bring the vinegar, 2 cups water, sugar, salt, and ginger to a boil. Meanwhile, in a small skillet over medium heat, toast the peppercorns, cloves, and star anise for 60 to 90 seconds, until they begin to smell toasty and fragrant. Remove from the heat and add to the brine. Let cool slightly. Place the preferred vegetable in a nonreactive container (or divide among canning jars) and pour the brine over to submerge. Let cool and refrigerate overnight before using (or process in a hot water bath for extended shelf life). **MAKES about 8 cups brine**

Summer Pickle Brine

4 cups white wine vinegar

½ cup sugar

¾ cup kosher salt

1 tablespoon pickling spice

4 cups ice

6 cloves garlic

2 ounces fresh dill broken into pieces (optional)

1 jalapeño, thinly sliced

In a large saucepot over high heat, bring the vinegar, 4 cups water, sugar, salt, and pickling spice to a boil. Remove from the heat and add the ice. Place the garlic, dill, jalapeño and preferred vegetable in a nonreactive container (or divide among canning jars) and pour the warm brine over to cover. Let cool and refrigerate overnight before using (or process in a hot water bath for extended shelf life). **MAKES about 8 cups brine**

I brine when I want to raise moisture in an ingredient and season it all the way through; **I cure when I want to lower moisture in an ingredient** and intensify the meaty flavor.

I use a cure when I'm working with red meats like pork, lamb, or venison or gamy birds like duck or guinea fowl. I also cure when I'm looking to lower the moisture level for preservation, like with dry-cured fish such as gravlax. Curing is basically brining without the water: I make a mixture of salt and sugar (with other aromatics depending on how I'm feeling that day) and rub the protein with this salt-sugar mixture. Then I wrap it and let it sit for up to a day (or even more).

Poole's Cure

1½ cups kosher salt

½ cup sugar

Zest of 1 orange

3 cloves garlic, thinly sliced

2 fresh bay leaves, thinly sliced

1 tablespoon fresh thyme leaves

½ teaspoon chile flakes

This all-purpose cure has a few aromatics thrown in to do double duty: removing moisture while also adding flavor. Take care to place a tray or plate under anything that you're curing, to catch any liquid that is drawn out by the cure. **MAKES about 2 cups**

Blend all of the ingredients together in a food processor until just aromatic and well combined. The cure will keep for up to 1 month in a lidded container in the refrigerator.

Herb Sachet

If you asked Lauren, one of our former sous chefs at Poole's, what this book should be called, *Everything Has a Sachet* might be her answer. We use herb sachets a lot when simmering or stewing something because they imbue the dish with aromatic flavors without letting the bits of herbs interrupt the texture. They also impart aromatic flavors into dishes without having you encounter pops of the herb itself. It's a really thoughtful way of scenting dishes with beautiful contributing flavors. Wrapping everything in cheesecloth makes it easy to yank it out when you're ready—no fishing around for that single garlic clove or thyme sprig in a saucepot of tomato soup.

The contents of the sachet stay more or less the same: fresh thyme, fresh bay, peppercorn, and garlic. This is a versatile combination, one that will work with a wide array of recipes. Try adding a sachet to your next batch of chicken soup or pot of beans. You can, of course, rock your sachet with flavors as you see fit.

I've included two sizes of sachet here, large and small, to be used depending on what you're making.

SMALL SACHET

4 medium thyme sprigs

½ fresh bay leaf

1 clove garlic

1 teaspoon black peppercorns

LARGE SACHET

8 medium thyme sprigs

1 bay leaf

2 cloves garlic

2 teaspoons black peppercorns

To make the sachet, cut a medium square of cheesecloth. Place the ingredients in the center of the square and tie the edges of the cloth together into a small bundle to secure (you could also tie with butcher's twine).

Lemon

There's almost no recipe on the planet that can't benefit from either a squeeze of lemon juice or a few scrapes of lemon zest. When I season foods with lemon juice, most of the time it's less about adding the flavor of lemon and more about elevating the existing flavors of the plate. I use both lemon juice and lemon zest (finely grated, on a rasp grater) in equal measure. One important distinction: I usually add lemon juice right before a dish is ready to be served, after it's been removed from a heat source, because direct heat can dim its flavor. Lemon zest, on the other hand, only brightens when exposed to heat, so it's great to use for seasoning during cooking. If you're not already in the habit of doing so, add lemons to every grocery list you make—even just one or two. They should be something you reach for as often as salt.

Oil

There are plenty of debates surrounding vegetable oil, a staple in any kitchen. We use a local non-GMO canola oil at Poole's for anything that requires a high smoke point (sautéing and frying), but any neutral vegetable oil, such as grapeseed, would work. We also use this oil for vinaigrettes, as it allows us to control which flavors we'd like to bring to the forefront. If we're specifically looking for the fruity, grassy flavor of olive oil, we'll often do a split of the two. Our favorite extra-virgin olive oil for drizzling and dressing is made of Arbequina olives. It has a green, nutty flavor, reminiscent of unripened bananas.

Butter

Cold butter in a hot sauce does more than add the flavor of butter to the dish. Instead, what I'm usually looking for is the velvety emulsion that the cold butter creates when swirled into a hot pot of brothy goodness.

A **compound butter** is just butter that has been spiked with another ingredient—a flavored butter. The two that we reach for most at Poole's are roasted garlic butter (affectionately shortened to as "Rogar" by our cooks) and porcini butter. I use the former to add a pinch of sweetness and depth to dishes that feel flat. I use porcini butter to bring a tone of earthiness to a sauce that's too bright and lacks follow-through or needs to connect to the origin of what it's complementing. Both butters deliver what I like to refer to as "backbone."

The other great thing about compound butter is that it can last for several months in the freezer, so you might want to double these recipes.

Roasted Garlic Butter (Rogar)

3 heads garlic (about 5 ounces)

1 tablespoon neutral vegetable oil

1 cup unsalted butter, at room temperature

Preheat a convection oven to 375°F (or a regular oven to 400°F). Slice off the tip and tail of each head of garlic to expose the cloves and place, root ends down, in a small baking dish. Drizzle with the oil and cover tightly with foil. Transfer to the oven and roast for 1 hour and 15 minutes. Let cool slightly.

When the garlic is cool enough to handle, squeeze the cloves from their skins. Place the garlic in a food processor and puree until smooth. Using a plastic spatula, push the garlic through a fine-mesh sieve set over a bowl.

In the bowl of a stand mixer fitted with the paddle attachment, add the butter and garlic puree and beat on medium speed until completely combined, about 5 minutes. Scoop into lidded containers and store in the refrigerator, up to 2 weeks, or freeze for up to 3 months. **MAKES about 1 cup**

Porcini Butter

1 ounce dried porcini mushrooms

1 cup unsalted butter, at room temperature

In a small saucepan, combine the dried mushrooms with just enough water to cover them. Bring to a boil; reduce to a simmer and cook on low heat for 45 minutes to an hour. There should still be a bit of liquid left in the pan. If not, add a splash of water.

Transfer the mushrooms and any remaining cooking liquid to a blender and puree on high speed until a thick, smooth paste forms. Spread the puree on a baking sheet lined with parchment paper and refrigerate until completely chilled.

In the bowl of a stand mixer fitted with the paddle attachment, beat the butter and mushroom puree until thoroughly incorporated, about 5 minutes. Scoop the butter into a lidded container and store in the refrigerator for up to 2 weeks, or freeze for up to 3 months. **MAKES about 1 cup**

Mayonnaise

You may not consider mayonnaise a method of seasoning yet, but if I have my way, you will. For the purposes of this book, I'm referring to mayonnaise made from scratch (though in general I am 100 percent in favor of a little Duke's from the jar). At Poole's (and at home), I make mayo with a noticeable punch of strong vinegar, usually either malt or cider vinegar, which delivers acid—the great uplifter of flavor—and perfect silky texture.

In addition to its unparalleled status as sidekick to fried food, mayo is the ultimate binder, holding together so many beautiful ingredients in dishes ranging from deviled eggs to pimento cheese. Making it from scratch allows you to control the flavor, tailoring it to whatever you're pairing it with.

Basic Cider Mayo

1 large egg yolk

½ teaspoon sea salt

1 teaspoon Dijon mustard

¼ cup cider vinegar

1½ cups neutral vegetable oil

In a food processor, puree the egg yolk, salt, mustard, and vinegar. With the motor running, slowly drizzle in the oil until thick and emulsified. Store in a lidded container in the refrigerator for up to 7 days.

MAKES about 1½ cups

Basic Malt Mayo

1 large egg yolk

½ teaspoon sea salt

1 teaspoon Dijon mustard

¼ cup malt vinegar

1½ cups neutral vegetable oil

In a food processor, puree the egg yolk, salt, mustard, and vinegar. With the motor running, slowly drizzle in the oil until thick and emulsified. Store in a lidded container in the refrigerator for up to 7 days.

MAKES about 1½ cups

Stocks

Outside of an accompaniment to meat, I don't utilize much stock in my cooking. As you'll find in the vegetable chapter, most of our veggies meet their fate in oil, herbs, and wine, or by way of the sear of a cast-iron pan. I also religiously believe that the finest potlikker comes from the peas, beans, and greens themselves, displaying a true, liquid representation of the earth from which they were harvested, like nature's little vegetable boullion cubes.

Where stock becomes really important to me is as the backbone in dishes like pot pie (see page 196) and Duck Slick (page 183), or in the brightly wine-based jus that cuts through the rich meat of the Royale (page 209), producing its subsequent savory bread pudding base. I think that stocks take a good bit of time and space to pull off, so when I add them to a dish, I only want to do so if it takes the plate to the status of "next level"; reaching a flavor or texture we couldn't have successfully achieved without its presence.

I've included recipes for two stocks that we use in a handful of recipes in this book. I classify them as "rich" as they both get reduced considerably.

In both recipes, I call for dried black trumpet mushrooms. They add a deep earthiness to the stock that contributes to an extra richness. Access whatever mushrooms you can (I prefer dried, but fresh will work), aiming toward earthier varieties like cremini and porcini. One word of caution: avoid shiitake, as they have a specific flavor, almost a perfume, that is not fitting for all of the dishes.

Rich Poultry Stock

For my poultry stock, I save up my duck backbones and wing tips from making confit or other recipes, storing them in the freezer for future use. If I'm short (or out all together) on the amount I need to make the stock, I purchase chicken wings.

2 pounds meaty poultry bones, such as backbones, wings, or neck bones

2 cups white wine

2 tablespoons neutral vegetable oil

2 onions, each cut into 8 pieces

2 heads garlic, sliced across the equator

½ pound carrots, roughly chopped

½ bunch celery (about 6 stalks), roughly chopped

½ ounce dried black trumpet mushrooms

1 teaspoon black peppercorns

8 medium thyme sprigs

1 fresh bay leaf, torn

Preheat a convection oven to 400°F (or a regular oven to 425°F). Grease a rimmed baking sheet with neutral vegetable oil. Place the bones on the pan, transfer to the oven, and roast for 40 minutes. Transfer the bones to a cutting board and, while the baking sheet is still very hot, pour ¼ cup of the wine into the pan, using a wooden spoon to scrape up any browned bits. Set aside.

In a large stock pot, heat the oil over medium heat. Add the onions and garlic, cut side down, and cook, undisturbed, for 2 minutes. Stir and cook for another 3 minutes, until the onions are caramelized. Add the carrots and celery and cook, stirring, to caramelize, another 6 minutes. Add the trumpet mushrooms and stir to coat. Add the roasted chicken bones, the liquid from the baking sheet, the remaining 1¾ cups white wine, the peppercorns, the thyme, and the bay. Bring to a simmer and cook, stirring occasionally, until the liquid is almost completely evaporated, 20 minutes. Add 4 quarts water, bring to a boil, and reduce to a gentle simmer. Cover and cook on low heat for 6 hours (or overnight).

Uncover and simmer to reduce the stock until you have 2 quarts of strained liquid, about 60 to 90 minutes. Strain the stock, and let cool completely. Store in lidded containers. The stock will keep in the refrigerator for 4 to 5 days, or in the freezer for 6 months. **MAKES 2 quarts**

Rich Beef Stock

This recipe calls for soup bones (typically cut from the beef femur bone), which can be sourced from your butcher. They are usually pretty affordable, and if your butcher is the friendly sort, he or she will likely be willing to cut the bones into 2-inch sections for you (I like the access to the marrow in this size cut, and it allows me to caramelize more surface area). These bones are coated in tomato paste before roasting in the oven because soup bones tend to be super lean. The natural sugar in the concentrated tomato paste provides something to caramelize in the absence of meat or sinew.

2 pounds beef soup bones

2 tablespoons double concentrate tomato paste

2 cups red wine

2 tablespoons neutral vegetable oil

2 onions, each cut into 8 pieces

2 heads garlic, sliced across the equator

½ pound carrots, roughly chopped

½ bunch celery (about 6 stalks), roughly chopped

½ ounce dried black trumpet mushrooms

1 teaspoon black peppercorns

8 medium thyme sprigs

1 fresh bay leaf, torn

Preheat a convection oven to 400°F (or a regular oven to 425°F). Grease a rimmed baking sheet with neutral vegetable oil. Place the bones on the pan and coat with the tomato paste. Transfer to the oven and roast for 25 minutes. Transfer the bones to a cutting board and, while the baking sheet is still very hot, pour ¼ cup of the wine into the pan, using a wooden spoon to scrape up any browned bits. Set aside.

In a large stock pot, heat the oil over medium heat. Add the onions and garlic, cut side down, and cook, undisturbed, for 2 minutes. Stir and cook for another 3 minutes, until the onions are caramelized. Add the carrots and celery and cook, stirring, to caramelize, another 6 minutes. Add the trumpet mushrooms and stir to coat. Add the roasted beef bones, the liquid from the baking sheet, the remaining 1¾ cups red wine, the peppercorns, the thyme, and the bay. Bring to a simmer and cook, stirring occasionally, until the liquid is almost completely evaporated, 20 minutes. Add 6 quarts water, bring to a boil, and reduce to a gentle simmer. Cover and cook on low heat for 6 to 8 hours (or overnight).

Uncover and reduce until the strained liquid measures 2 quarts, about 1½ to 2 hours. Strain the liquid and let cool completely. Store in lidded containers. The stock will keep in the refrigerator for 4 to 5 days, or frozen for 6 months. **MAKES 2 quarts**

Back Pocket Recipes

It used to be the norm that cookbooks would have a "pantry" section where the author would outline the things you need to stock up on before you start cooking. These days, home cooks are a sophisticated bunch, so I'm assuming a little bit of proficiency. Rather than tell you how to do your grocery shopping, I'm sharing a few of my favorite prepped ingredients that will take pretty much any meal in an entirely new direction; think of it as Pantry 2.0. These recipes, titled "The Back Pocket," appear throughout the book. They can and should be utilized in a variety of ways (in addition to those outlined in each recipe). In my opinion, each of them justifies the effort it requires to whip them up in what it adds to your finished product, particularly since so many can be made ahead and refrigerated or frozen until you're ready to use them.

Counter Snacks

(THINGS THAT PEOPLE STAND AROUND AND EAT)

In most cookbooks, this chapter would probably be called Appetizers. But for me, a successful dish is something people want to eat at any point during the meal or make into a meal of its own. So let's rip the "appetizer" tag off these and eat them whenever and wherever we choose—so long as they're shared.

One of the most prominent features of the Poole's dining room is the bar, which curves around like two side-by-side horseshoes. Before it was a bar, though, this swooping surface was the counter, a fixture of any classic diner or luncheonette. Historically, counters were places to enjoy a quick, unfussy meal, or a place to grab a cup of coffee and a snack, sometimes without even sitting down. My first memory of a counter is of the one in my childhood home. As a child, I would perch at one of the seats at our kitchen counter, where I had the best view of my parents as they shared dominion over the stove. Behind me, friends and family would gather, socialize, and give toasts while they waited for my parents' creations to emerge.

It was laid-back, warm, and welcoming. Snacks were handed out by whoever was cooking, or plopped directly into your mouth by a friend or relative excited for you to taste something delicious. I think back to those gatherings and that sense of intimacy with every plate we set on the worn Formica of the Poole's Diner counter.

The recipes in this chapter harness that same energy; they are intimate, informal, eat-with-your-hands-style dishes that can fit into any circumstance. On a personal level, these are the foods that taught me how to love to eat and, by extension, to cook. They conjure some of my deepest, warmest memories from a time long before I imagined food as a career.

It pays homage to dishes like the humble deviled egg, which taught me to have confidence in my own cooking voice, or oysters Rockefeller, one of my father's favorite dishes, which helped me embrace the ingredients of the South. These remain some of the most personal recipes in my playbook.

Each time I'm making Fried Eggplant with Burnt Honey Aioli (page 44), I think about my father, Fox, teaching me to make his eggplant Parmesan, keeping my right hand dry for flour and bread crumbs as my left hand dipped slices of eggplant into the wet egg batter. When I peel the shrimp for Pickled Shrimp with Roasted Tomato Cocktail Sauce (page 55), I think back to childhood trips to the coast and the peel-and-eat shrimp that gave us implicit permission to eat with our hands. I hope these dishes tap into your own memories and are among the dishes you and your family and friends will share.

Pimento Cheese

In the South, pimento cheese is a little bit like barbecue: everyone swears theirs is the best. But pimento cheese didn't originate in the South; it has roots in the industrial food revolution in New York. Sometime around the 1950s, Southerners claimed it, giving pimento cheese its now-permanent residence below the Mason-Dixon Line.

The Poole's version of pimento cheese is based on the recipe of my "grand-godmother"—my godmother's mother, Marge France. Marge was the wife of Forest "Bud" France, a decorated army lieutenant colonel and a train master for the B&O Railroad (he was the one who kept the trains running on time). Their only child, my godmother, Suzette, had no children, and Bud and Marge took on the role of grandparents to me and my brother, Zak. We called them Uncle Bud and Aunt Marge, and in many ways I felt closer to them than to my biological grandparents.

Uncle Bud was an avid golfer and often took me out with him, armed with two sets of clubs and a tiny cooler of homemade pimento cheese sandwiches packed by Aunt Marge. Halfway through a day on the links, Uncle Bud would pull the golf cart under a shade tree where we'd eat the sandwiches. For me, pimento cheese is inextricably linked with the memory of the salty South Carolina summer heat, the smell of the freshly cut grass, and the outlines of my small fingers impressed in the cool white bread.

Marge's pimento cheese was so different from the soft, subtly sweet version I ate at home in North Carolina (bought from our local grocer, Musten & Crutchfield). The ingredients were definitive, yet harmonious: finely grated sharp cheddar that held its form, a healthy spike of vinegar, and mayonnaise in a perfect supporting role. The pimento peppers in Marge's pimento cheese even seemed to sing a little more.

Bud and Marge came to South Carolina from Chillicothe, Ohio. I was mesmerized by their accents—especially how Marge pronounced the word *ornery* (which I occasionally was). Bud and Marge always treated me like an adult, and I loved that. I loved even more that they always treated me like I belonged to them, no matter how ornery I was. Only now, as I write this, do I realize that my pimento cheese is more connected to the North than the South, by way of Chillicothe, Aunt Marge, and Uncle Bud.

Continued

Pimento cheese is a constant on the Poole's menu. We use three-year-aged cheddar, punchy cider vinegar, lots of toasted Tellicherry pepper, and red peppers that we roast ourselves, in order to get the texture just right.

We often welcome friends and first-timers to the restaurant with our pimento cheese. We jar it up and send it in the mail as a thank-you to folks who have hosted us in their kitchens, or to folks who have just been nice to us in general. We've even used it to solidify an apology or two. It tells a story, without interrupting anyone's conversation. It belongs to us, and to everyone. Every time I make it, I am reminded of those sandwiches under the shade tree, and of the importance of chosen family. **MAKES 6½ cups; enough for 18 sandwiches**

PIMENTO CHEESE

2 small to medium red bell peppers (14 ounces)

¼ cup cider vinegar

1 cup Basic Cider Mayo (page 21)

2 tablespoons finely grated red onion

1 tablespoon finely ground toasted black pepper (see page 13)

½ teaspoon sea salt

2 tablespoons hot sauce (I use a combination of Tabasco and Texas Pete)

1¼ pounds three-year-aged cheddar, finely grated (we use Hook's, from Wisconsin)

15 ounces sharp white cheddar, finely grated

Crostini, for serving

To roast the peppers, place them directly over a high gas flame. Using metal tongs to safely rotate the peppers, char the entire surface of each pepper. My final step in this process is to balance the pepper on its curvy stem end on the grate of the burner to char that part. This ensures the best yield. (If you don't have a gas range, roast the peppers under an oven broiler set on high; rotate them with metal tongs so they char evenly.)

Transfer the peppers to a metal bowl and cover with plastic wrap. Let sit for 15 minutes. Use a dish towel to gently rub off the skins of the peppers; don't run them under water, as this will wash away some of the flavor. Remove the stems and seeds, and finely dice the peppers. You should have about ¾ cup.

To pickle the peppers, in a small bowl, combine the diced peppers and cider vinegar; refrigerate overnight. (Or, if you can't wait, let sit at room temperature at least 3 hours.)

The next day, combine the peppers and their vinegar with the mayo, onion, pepper, salt, and hot sauce in a large bowl; mix well. Combine the cheeses in a separate bowl and mix well. Add the pepper mixture to the cheese and mix to combine. Let the mixture chill in the refrigerator for 1 hour before serving; it should be thick but still spreadable.

Serve with crostini, or jar it up and refrigerate it for up to 7 days.

Classic Deviled Eggs

Deviled eggs are another staple from my childhood, and from the childhoods of most Southerners. At weddings, family reunions, and funerals, there'd always be a table lined with plates and Tupperware carriers of deviled eggs, all laden with halved egg whites, their hollows unceremoniously stuffed with mounds of mustard-yellow filling. More than likely, a generous dusting of paprika had, in the journey from kitchen to table, transformed from garnish to a fused element of the egg itself. These plates of eggs stand in my memory as a thing of beauty.

This dish has always been special to me, but as a young, not-yet-secure cook, I was embarrassed at the prospect of its being representative of my "cuisine" and would never have dreamed of putting it on a menu. Then I visited Gabrielle Hamilton's restaurant, Prune, in New York City. As I devoured my first bistro-born deviled egg, I remember thinking, "It's okay to serve these in a restaurant? Wow, that's so cool!"

I often describe my cooking as an exploded-view drawing of simple classics: I focus on every detail and ingredient with care and respectful imagination. My version of the deviled egg may be the perfect example of this philosophy. The details and cuts are sharp, the condiments are housemade, and the egg yolk is fluffy and buttery. **MAKES 24; serves 6 as an appetizer**

12 large eggs

½ cup Countertop Crème Fraîche (page 159), or sour cream

1 tablespoon minced cornichons, plus 2 tablespoons cornichon juice

1 tablespoon Dijon mustard

1 tablespoon plus 1 teaspoon Basic Cider Mayo (page 21)

2 tablespoons minced shallot

2 tablespoons unsalted butter, melted

½ teaspoon sea salt

Continued

Place the eggs in a medium saucepan and cover with 1 inch of cold water. Bring to a rolling boil over high heat. When the water is boiling, cover the pan and turn off the heat. Let sit for 8 minutes. Meanwhile, fill a bowl with ice water. Drain the eggs and immediately transfer to the ice water. Let sit for 10 minutes, then drain the eggs and dry them well. Peel the eggs carefully and slice them in half lengthwise. Remove the yolks, keeping the egg white halves intact.

In a food processor, combine the yolks, crème fraîche, cornichon juice, and mustard and puree until smooth. Pass the yolk mixture through a fine-mesh sieve into a medium bowl. Fold in the mayo, shallot, cornichons, butter, salt, and 10 cranks of pepper. Mix well to combine and transfer to the refrigerator to set for one hour. (You can prepare the eggs up to this point 1 day ahead: store the whites in the refrigerator, cut side down

Black pepper in a mill

6 chives, cut into ½-inch lengths,
    for garnish (optional)

Ground piment d'Espelette,
    for garnish (optional)

Pickled green tomato slivers,
    for garnish (optional)

note: Here's a trick to make it
easier to peel your hard-boiled
eggs: prick the bottom of each egg
with a straight pin before adding
to the water to boil.

on a paper towel–lined plate covered with plastic wrap; store the filling
separately in the refrigerator, covered with plastic wrap pressed directly
on the surface.)

When you're ready to fill the egg white halves, line them up on a
work surface or arrange them on a serving platter. Place the egg filling
in a pastry bag fitted with a star tip and pipe the filling into the egg white
halves. Garnish with chives, piment d'Espelette, pickled green tomato
slices, or whatever strikes you as delicious.

The eggs, once assembled, are best eaten on the day they're prepared.

Confit for Duck or Rabbit

The French technique of cooking duck or chicken or rabbit in a low-heat bath of fat is quite a project, but it makes the most beautifully tender, rich meat on earth. I tackle the task at home by taking a confit day just three or four times a year and making enough to freeze and hold me through a few months of cooking.

Use confit to whip up a quick batch of rillettes (see right) or to stuff into poblanos (see page 219). I also love to fold confit into gravy to be ladled over biscuits for the most decadent brunch dish ever. It's beautiful when laced through frisée in a simple salad, and it transforms a bowl of white beans into an elegant meal (top with a bit of *gremolata*, see page 226, for balance). **MAKES 2 cups**

1 whole duck, backbone and wings removed, or 1 whole rabbit

2 tablespoons plus 2 teaspoons Poole's Cure (page 17)

5⅓ cups rendered duck fat

note: As you use the confit, you can continue to strain and reuse the duck fat until it becomes salty to the taste.

Place the duck or rabbit on a work surface and rub all over with the Poole's Cure. Set on a baking sheet and refrigerate for 24 hours.

Rinse the duck or rabbit and pat dry. Preheat a convection oven to 225°F (or a regular oven to 250°F). Place the duck or rabbit in a Dutch oven and cover with the duck fat. Cover with a tight-fitting lid, place in the oven, and cook for 3 hours, or until very tender and falling apart. Uncover and let cool for 2 hours, then remove the meat from the liquid.

Strain the fat through a fine-mesh sieve and reserve. Pull the meat from the bones and place in a bowl; save the bones and carcass for making stock or discard. Unless you're using the meat immediately, place it in a lidded container and cover with the strained duck fat. You can refrigerate the confit, covered, for up to 7 days or freeze for up to 6 months.

Chicken Liver Mousse

Liver can be a tough sell. For some, it's about the fear of the unknown; for others it's not-so-fond memories of economical, but often over-cooked, liver and onions. I too grew up with a weekly dose of that dish, and as an adult free to cook as I choose, it's one food memory I have no desire to re-create. Chicken liver mousse, though? That's a different story.

I have made several different versions of liver mousse, but this version is inspired by Scott Howell of Nana's in Durham, North Carolina. His recipe is delicious and elegantly simple, with a basic equation that even I, never much for math, was able to memorize.

Once cooked, livers can sometimes become a bit grainy. This recipe safeguards the silkiness of the livers by emulsifying them with cold butter before the mousse is cooked. Between its mellow, rich taste and its easy preparation, this a great opening argument for anyone on the fence about liver. **MAKES two 8-ounce jars; serves 16 to 20 as a party snack**

8 ounces chicken livers, trimmed of sinews

Milk, for soaking the livers

1½ teaspoons orange zest

1 teaspoon fresh thyme leaves

1 tablespoon Grand Marnier

Black pepper in a mill

4 tablespoons unsalted butter, at room temperature

4 tablespoons rendered duck fat, at room temperature

3 large egg yolks

1½ teaspoons sea salt

¼ cup heavy cream

Excellent Dijon mustard, for serving

Assorted pickles and jams, for serving

Crostini or crackers, for serving

Rinse the chicken livers in cold water and pat dry. Place them in a container and cover with milk so that they are completely submerged (this draws out blood and impurities). Cover and refrigerate overnight.

Combine the zest, thyme, Grand Marnier, and a few cranks of pepper in a small container. Cover and refrigerate overnight.

Preheat a convection oven to 275°F (or a regular oven to 300°F).

Drain the livers, rinse, and pat dry; discard the milk. In a food processor, combine the livers, butter, and duck fat and puree until emulsified and completely smooth, 5 minutes. Add the egg yolks and salt and pulse a few times just to combine. Push the puree through a fine-mesh sieve. Strain the Grand Marnier through a fine-mesh strainer set over a bowl and discard the solids. Fold the Grand Marnier into the liver mixture, along with the cream. Divide the mixture among two 8-ounce heatproof jars; fill up to just below the lip of each jar. Cover the jars with foil. Place the jars in a baking pan and fill the pan with water to reach halfway up the sides of the jars.

Bake until an instant thermometer inserted in the center of the jars reads 165°F, about 30 minutes. Uncover the jars and remove from the pan. Let cool completely, then cover with plastic wrap and refrigerate until chilled. The mousse will keep in the refrigerator for 5 days.

Serve cold with Dijon, your favorite pickles and jam, and crostini.

Black Pepper Parmesan Popcorn

In my house, popcorn is an all-occasion food, as suitable for a large dinner party as it is for a lazy night on the couch. It's familiar, it's fun, and it brings people together in easy conversation. What's not to love?

While I'll always have a soft spot for oversize movie-theater kernels, I've become a convert to newly available heirloom varieties of popcorn, like Indigo or Yellow Flint from Geechie Boy Mill. They have distinctive flavor notes, and they tell an important alternative story to the big-ag version of corn.

Like many things, when you start with beautiful base materials, it's best to keep it simple. This recipe has only a few ingredients, so use the best quality you can find. That said, it can be MacGyvered easily with whatever you have available. It's a staple of the annual ski weekend I take in Vail, Colorado, so I can attest it'll stand up to even the most sparse of vacation-house pantries. As a snack this recipe will feed 2 really hungry skiers or 4 to 6 people with normal appetites.

MAKES 2 quarts

¼ cup popcorn kernels, preferably an heirloom variety

¼ cup olive oil

1 tablespoon Dijon mustard

¼ teaspoon sea salt

Black pepper in a mill

¼ cup finely grated Parmigiano-Reggiano

Place the popcorn kernels in a paper lunch bag and fold over the top of the bag three times in 1-inch folds. Place upright in the microwave for 1 minute 45 seconds, or until the sound of popping slows down to 3 to 5 seconds between each pop.

In a large bowl, combine the olive oil, mustard, salt, and about 40 cranks of the pepper mill. Whisk together (it won't entirely emulsify), then use a rubber spatula to spread the mixture around the sides of the bowl (it'll thicken up into a paste as you spread; this is fine). Add the popcorn to the bowl and use a spatula to fold the popcorn against the coated walls of the bowl. Make sure the popcorn is well coated. Add the cheese in three batches, using your hands to incorporate each addition before adding more. Serve immediately.

Fried Eggplant with Burnt Honey Aioli

Eggplant Parmesan was one of my father's go-to dishes, and he converted many of my childhood friends to the magic of the vegetable this way. They would squint their eyes at the mention of it, probably wishing for a hot dog instead, only to try a bite and—inevitably—love it.

My dad, Fox, always assigned me the three-bin task of carefully dipping the eggplant slices into flour, then egg, then bread crumbs, with my dominant hand for the dry ingredients and my left hand for the wet egg bath. He'd then fry them to a wondrous state of golden crispness. As he focused his attention on building the layers in the baking dish, I would snag a slice of the just-fried eggplant, crispy on the outside and sweet and creamy at the center. Even in its sauceless, unadorned state, it was magical, a brilliant showcase of the eggplant's best features.

This dish elaborates on my early fascination with those fried eggplant slices by treating them like French fries and taking the tomato sauce and cheese out of the equation. Cutting the eggplant into fry form encourages dipping, and the aioli plays on the natural friendship between eggplant and honey. Chef Sean Brock inspired the burnt honey I use in the mayo; it channels a crème caramel–like depth, echoing the sweetness that the quick fry has romanced to the surface of the eggplant. **SERVES 4**

BURNT HONEY AIOLI

¼ cup plus 2 tablespoons honey

1 cup Basic Cider Mayo
    (page 21)

1 medium globe eggplant
    (12 to 14 ounces)

Sea salt

4 large eggs, beaten

1 cup all-purpose flour

2 cups panko

Neutral vegetable oil, for frying

To make the aioli, in a medium saucepan over high heat, bring the honey to a boil. Reduce to a simmer and let the honey cook until it is reduced by two-thirds (it will be a dark amber in color), about 8 minutes. Remove from the heat and let cool completely. Whisk together with the mayo and refrigerate until ready to use. The aioli can be made 3 days in advance.

Line a baking sheet with parchment paper. Peel and trim the eggplant and slice it into ¾-by-5-inch spears—like steak fries. Arrange the eggplant in a single layer on the lined baking sheet. Sprinkle with ½ teaspoon salt and let sit for 20 minutes to leach out some of the eggplant's liquid.

In a shallow bowl, whisk together the eggs and ¼ cup water. In a second shallow bowl, stir together the flour and 1 teaspoon salt. Put the panko in a third bowl.

Pat the eggplant spears dry. Dredge each piece in the flour mixture (shake off the extra), then the egg mixture (switch hands so one hand stays dry), then finally coat them well in the panko. Arrange the eggplant on a parchment-lined baking sheet in a single, even layer. (You can make the eggplant up to this point and freeze it for up to 1 month; place the baking sheet, uncovered, in the freezer for 1 hour, then transfer the spears to a resealable plastic bag and freeze until needed. There's no need to thaw beforehand: you can add the frozen eggplant directly to the hot oil when you're ready to fry it.)

Fill a heavy-bottomed pan halfway with oil and heat to 350°F on a deep-fry thermometer. Working in batches, add a few of the spears to the oil and fry until golden brown, about 5 minutes. Transfer to a paper towel–lined plate and sprinkle with salt. Repeat with the remaining spears.

Serve immediately, with a dish of burnt honey aioli for dipping.

Tuna Tartare with Piment d'Espelette and Cucumber

There are some fairly simple things required for making successful tuna tartare: super fresh fish, a good sharp blade, and a willingness to taste as you go. The texture of the dish is dependent on how the fish is cut, so take your time to create a uniform dice. I suggest slicing the tuna into ¼-inch-thick slabs, then placing them on a baking sheet in the freezer—not to freeze the tuna but to get it very, very cold, which makes it easier to dice. Make vertical slices, matching the thickness of each slab, and then horizontal slices of the same width. Consider the perfect dice demystified. Your knife game is now pro style.

I got the idea for fried quinoa from New Orleans chef Justin Devillier. We were cooking at an event together, and I watched in awe as he studded hand-minced steak tartare with handfuls of the stuff (texture! texture! texture!). I've done the same ever since.

Raw cucumber slices provide a fresh and crisp vehicle for the tuna, but I also love grilling the cucumbers lightly on one side before topping with the tuna tartare, especially in summer when the grill is often already warmed up.

Tuna tartare is endlessly versatile. Use it as a jumping-off point for your own experiments. I've been known to add avocado, malt mayo, oil-cured olives, or pickled garlic. **SERVES 4 to 6**

1 English cucumber

8 ounces sushi-grade tuna loin, finely diced (see headnote) and kept cold

Sea salt

½ teaspoon ground piment d'Espelette

Juice of 1 lemon

2 teaspoons minced shallot

1 tablespoon fresh chives, minced

2 tablespoons olive oil

1 tablespoon Crispy Quinoa (page 48)

Place a medium bowl (preferably metal) in the freezer to chill. Cut a 3-inch-long section off the end of the cucumber, then remove the seedy center (by scraping it out gently with the tip of the spoon) and discard. Mince this section and set aside; slice the rest of the cucumber into ½-inch-thick rounds.

In the cold mixing bowl, stir together the tuna, minced cucumber, ¼ teaspoon sea salt, piment d'Espelette, lemon juice, shallot, and chives. Stir until mixture is well combined. Next, gently stir in the olive oil, then fold in the quinoa.

Grab a spoon and taste. Adjust the seasoning to your preference and keep seasoning and tasting until you nail it. Arrange the cucumber rounds on a platter and season them lightly with sea salt. Spoon a heaping teaspoon of tartare on the center of each. Serve immediately.

Crispy Quinoa

I'm the type of person who lines my tuna fish sandwich with potato chips. I love the texture of a little crunch, and fried quinoa satisfies that craving.

This recipe started out as part of a tuna tartare we were serving at Poole's. I wasn't going to include it in this book because it seemed like a lot of work for such a tiny component of a single dish. But then I made it at home one day, and having a container of the stuff hanging around was like Christmas morning and a day at the beach all wrapped in one—that is to say, amazing. I threw a handful of it into kale salad; I used it as a garnish for chicken soup; I sprinkled it on wedges of roasted sweet potato and over a plate of scrambled eggs. And the best part? It lasts for up to 1 month in a lidded plastic container, retaining all its crunch and flavor. Bye-bye croutons, bye-bye bread crumbs; hello crispy quinoa. **MAKES 2½ cups**

2 tablespoons Dijon mustard

1 teaspoon honey

½ cup white wine vinegar

Sea salt

1½ cups extra-virgin olive oil

Black pepper in a mill

1 cup red quinoa

Neutral vegetable oil, for frying

Bring a large pot of salted water to a boil.

In a mixing bowl, whisk together the mustard, honey, vinegar, and a pinch of salt. While continuing to whisk, drizzle in the olive oil to emulsify. Finish with a few cranks of pepper and set aside.

Cook the quinoa in the boiling water until fully cooked (the germ will have separated from the seeds), about 15 minutes. Drain the quinoa and add directly to the mixing bowl with the vinaigrette; stir to combine. Let the quinoa marinate in the refrigerator for 2 hours or up to overnight. Drain the quinoa in a fine-mesh sieve, shaking to remove any excess liquid. Lay out on paper towels to dry completely.

In a medium saucepan—one that is wide enough to insert a small fine-mesh sieve but not so wide that you need a ton of oil—heat 3 inches of oil until it reaches 380°F on a deep-fry thermometer. Transfer the quinoa to a fine-mesh sieve and lower it into the fryer so that the quinoa is completely submerged; do this in batches if it works better for your setup. Fry for 1 minute, or until the quinoa is crispy. Lay the quinoa out on a baking sheet lined with paper towels and season with salt. Let the quinoa cool completely, and transfer to a lidded container lined with a paper towel (which will absorb any excess oil). The quinoa will keep in the pantry for 1 month.

Pork Ribs with Mustard Sorghum Sauce

I love a pork rib. It's such a delicious delivery of meat-on-the-bone, and it comes with a handle! I often hear people compliment ribs by saying they're "fall-off-the-bone" tender—and therefore delicious. This is a bit of a contradiction to me. I believe a proper rib should be full of flavor and ever-so-slightly tender, but it's the connection to the bone that makes it interesting. Anyone can braise a rib into fall-off-the-bone submission, but to walk the line where perfect texture and flavor meet is the real challenge.

To hit the sweet spot, I use lessons learned from all of my pit-master pals (and teammates from the Fatback Collective, a group of chefs, writers, and pitmasters who come together to support our collective communities and learn about new approaches to cooking) for delicious whole-hog barbecue: start slow and low, and fire it up at the end. This recipe uses a three-step process—the cure, the slow roast, and the glaze—and the time associated with each has a major payoff in the final product. The combination of good Dijon mustard and sweet sorghum brings out the rich flavor and texture of the ribs while creating a beautifully caramelized glaze over the meat. **SERVES 4 as a main course or 8 to 12 as a snack**

2 racks St. Louis–style pork ribs (about 4 pounds total)

2 tablespoons Poole's Cure (page 17)

Sea salt

Black pepper in a mill

½ cup Dijon mustard

¼ cup sorghum (I like Muddy Pond)

Place the rib racks on a work surface and rub all over with the cure. Wrap each rack tightly with plastic wrap, place on a rimmed baking sheet (the cure will leach liquid from the meat, so you want something to catch it in case it leaks), and refrigerate for 12 hours. Unwrap the racks and rinse off the cure; pat dry with paper towels.

Preheat a convection oven to 250°F (or a regular oven to 275°F). Season the racks lightly with salt and pepper. Wrap each rack in foil and place side by side on a baking sheet; bake for 2 hours. Remove from the oven and let rest, still wrapped in foil, for 30 minutes.

While the ribs are resting, whisk together the mustard and sorghum in a medium bowl. Coat the ribs in the sauce and place on a foil-lined baking sheet under the broiler until caramelized, about 5 minutes. Alternatively, you could caramelize the ribs on a grill over medium-high heat.

Slice the racks into individual ribs and serve hot with lots of paper towels.

TNT Chicken Livers with Hot Hot Aioli and Pickle Relish

I came to know one of my favorite cities, Nashville, through two chefs who have played a large role in defining its food scene: my friends Tandy Wilson of City House and Tyler Brown of Southall. Tandy and Tyler have made it their mission to show off all the greatness Nashville has to offer. They call their combined forces "TNT," and they bring every bit of the big-bang impact the name suggests. Their partnerships have ranged from demos and dinners at food festivals around the country to fund-raisers for important charitable causes.

I fell in love with Nashville as Tandy and Tyler shared its incredible joints and dives with me. One of these was Prince's Hot Chicken, which is famous for one dish: pieces of chicken, batter fried hotter than hell, with cayenne pepper everywhere you can imagine it (including in the frying oil), served on a slice of white bread with a pile of dill pickle chips on top. The pickle juice weeps its way down through the crispy chicken and collects in a pool on the cooling white bread, creating a vortex of spice, schmaltz, and vinegar. Epic.

This recipe gives chicken livers the Prince's treatment in a snack version of the original. I use a brown paper shopping bag to coat the livers in the flour-and-cayenne dredge; it ensures that all of the nooks and crannies of the livers are well seasoned. You can eat these as is, topped with a dollop of mayo and relish, or serve them with crostini—or on slices of white bread (the cheaper the better) if you're a hot chicken purist. It's an ode to TNT and to what they taught me about Nashville and its hot chicken—and about loving and advocating for the places we call home. **SERVES 8 as a snack**

Continued

1 pound chicken livers,
    trimmed of sinews

2 cups milk

1 cup buttermilk

3 cups all-purpose flour

1 tablespoon cayenne pepper

2 teaspoons sea salt

1 tablespoon freshly ground
    black pepper

Neutral vegetable oil, for frying

HOT HOT AIOLI

2 teaspoons cayenne pepper

2 tablespoons red wine vinegar

1½ cups Basic Cider Mayo
    (page 21)

Sea salt

PICKLE RELISH

1 cup diced high-quality dill pickles
    (ideally homemade; see page 16)

2 shallots, minced

¼ cup olive oil

Sea salt

Black pepper in a mill

In a bowl, cover the livers with the milk and leave to soak in the refrigerator overnight. (This will pull out blood and impurities.)

To make the aioli, combine the cayenne and vinegar in a bowl and leave to stand for 20 minutes to bloom the cayenne. Whisk in the mayonnaise and season to taste with salt. You may refrigerate this aioli for up to 3 days, but it's best served fresh.

To make the pickle relish, combine the pickles, shallots, and olive oil in a bowl. Season with salt and pepper as needed. Some pickles may be vibrant enough to need no additional seasoning. Keep at room temperature for immediate use or refrigerate if preparing in advance. If you do prepare this in advance, allow it to come up to room temperature before serving.

To finish the livers, drain them well and pat them dry; discard the milk. Place them in a shallow bowl and cover them with the buttermilk. In a brown paper shopping bag, mix the flour, cayenne, salt, and pepper.

Line a baking sheet with a triple layer of paper towels. Heat ½ inch oil in a large cast-iron skillet over medium heat until it reaches 325°F on a deep-fry thermometer.

While the oil is heating, lift the livers from the buttermilk one by one, shaking off the excess buttermilk, and transfer them to the paper bag. Try to coat the livers with flour as you drop each one in the bag; this prevents them from sticking together.

Once all of the livers are in the bag, fold the top of the bag over two or three times and shake it vigorously. Transfer the livers one by one to the hot oil, working in batches so they don't touch one another. Be cautious! The livers tend to release a bit of liquid while cooking, which makes the oil pop. Keep a dry kitchen towel on hand to protect yourself while maneuvering the livers around the pan. As you see the edges of the livers browning, flip them with tongs. Once both sides are golden brown and crisp, 2 to 3 minutes on each side, remove the livers from the pan and place them on the lined baking sheet to drain.

I prefer to serve this family-style: place a generous dollop of aioli on a large platter and arrange the livers in a pile on top of the aioli. Top with 3 spoonfuls of pickle relish and serve hot. You could also serve the livers next to a bowl of the aioli and have your guests dip.

Pickled Shrimp with Roasted Tomato Cocktail Sauce

I've learned many great lessons from my dear friend Alex Raij, chef of Txikito in New York City. On her first of many visits to cook with us in North Carolina, she shared with me the technique of briefly brining raw shrimp in iced salted water. It imparts perfect seasoning to the core of the shrimp, whereas if you add salt to the pan, it seasons only the exterior of the shrimp.

The pickling process here is more of a dressing than a means of preservation—a bright, punchy lift for the sweet, buttery shellfish. Feel free to take creative license here: switch up the spices to suit your taste. Since it's served cold, it's a great dish for preparing ahead of time.

The only nonvariable here is using all-natural, chemical-free shrimp. This recipe is built to magnify the flavors of the shrimp, so any muddy flavors will also be magnified. **SERVES 8**

2 cups white balsamic vinegar

¼ cup sugar

½ cup pickling spice

1 cup plus 2 tablespoons kosher salt

4 cups ice

2 pounds 26/30 count shrimp, peeled and deveined

COCKTAIL SAUCE

1 cup Roasted Tomatoes (page 162), chopped

½ shallot, minced

¼ cup prepared or freshly grated horseradish

Zest and juice of 1 lemon

2 tablespoons extra-virgin olive oil

½ cup tomato juice

¾ teaspoon sea salt

Black pepper in a mill

In a medium saucepan over medium heat, combine the vinegar, sugar, pickling spice, ¼ cup plus 2 tablespoons kosher salt, and 2 cups water. Bring to a boil, stirring until the salt and sugar have dissolved. Strain the liquid, discarding the solids, and let cool completely.

In a large bowl, whisk together ¾ cup kosher salt, 4 cups water, and the ice. Add the shrimp and brine for 20 minutes.

Meanwhile, in a medium saucepan over high heat, bring 3 cups water and the remaining ¾ cup of the salt to a boil.

Drain the shrimp and place in a heatproof metal bowl. Pour the boiling salted water over the shrimp and let sit, stirring occasionally, until the shrimp are opaque and cooked through, about 8 minutes. Drain, arrange the shrimp in an even layer on a baking sheet, and refrigerate until chilled.

When the shrimp are cold, dress them generously in the cooled pickling liquid and let them sit at room temperature for 30 minutes before serving.

To make the cocktail sauce, combine the tomatoes, shallot, horseradish, lemon zest and juice, olive oil, and tomato juice in a small bowl. Season with salt and freshly ground pepper. Serve the sauce either chilled or at room temperature with the pickled shrimp. The cocktail sauce can be prepared 1 day in advance and stored in the refrigerator.

Oysters Rock-a-Billy

Growing up, my family frequently vacationed on the Carolina coast, and we always sought out an oyster bar upon arrival. My party trick involved happily slurping raw oysters—something most kids abhorred—by the dozen, as the mystified adults around me gawked.

I still adore oysters on the half shell, particularly the briny, minerally ones from the East Coast. But I'm also a huge fan of baked and roasted oysters and have inherited a special love for the classic dish oysters Rockefeller from my father, a New Yorker. This recipe brings that dish into my geographical orbit, with ingredients I hold dear.

The oysters are best enjoyed straight from the oven, washed down with a can of ice-cold beer-flavored beer. **MAKES 48 oysters**

½ cup Roasted Tomatoes (page 162), minced

½ teaspoon minced shallot

2 tablespoons olive oil

Black pepper in a mill

Sea salt

2 tablespoons neutral vegetable oil

½ cup minced yellow onion

10 ounces turnip greens (about 1 bunch), roughly chopped

½ cup heavy cream

1 cup finely diced turnip root

4 dozen chubby East Coast oysters, on the half shell

¼ cup cornbread crumbs (see page 100)

note: If your oysters are super briny, avoid adding extra salt.

In a small bowl, combine the tomatoes, shallot, olive oil, 10 cranks of the pepper mill, and ¼ teaspoon salt. Set aside.

In a large, heavy-bottomed skillet, heat the oil over medium heat. Add the onion and cook until softened, about 3 minutes. Add the turnip greens and cook, stirring occasionally, until the greens are tender, about 4 minutes. Season with salt and remove from the heat. When the greens are cool enough to handle, squeeze any excess moisture from them; set aside.

In a small saucepan over medium heat, combine the cream, ¼ teaspoon salt, diced turnip root, and ½ cup water and bring to a simmer. Reduce the heat to low and simmer until the turnip is tender, about 12 minutes. Transfer the cream and turnip mixture to a food processor and pulse until it forms a paste. Add the reserved turnip greens and puree for 60 to 90 seconds. Taste and season according to the salt level of your oysters (see Note). Set aside. (The creamed turnip greens can be made up to 3 days in advance and stored in the refrigerator until ready to use.)

Preheat a convection oven to 400°F (or a regular oven to 425°F). Cover two rimmed baking sheets with a layer of rock salt to serve as a bed for the oysters. Arrange the oysters in their half shells on the rock salt. Season the oysters lightly with salt, then top each oyster with 1 teaspoon of the creamed turnip greens. Transfer the oysters to the oven and bake for 6 to 8 minutes, until the oysters just start to bubble around the edges.

Top each oyster with ½ teaspoon of the tomato relish and a pinch of cornbread crumbs. Serve immediately.

Pâte à Choux

Line cooks and state fairs have imagined a million ways to fry just about any ingredient you can think of. But in my mind, there's no better excuse for firing up the fryer than doughnuts.

Using the pâte à choux as a base, you can mix in any ingredients you like, from savory (think black-eyed peas or sweet potatoes) to sweet (coconut, pumpkin, or roasted banana would all be great). I've included two savory variations in this chapter (Crab Churros with Piquillo Pepper Mayo on page 60 and Turnip Green Fritters with Whipped Tahini on page 61) and one more twist in the dessert section (Zucchini Doughnuts with Mascarpone on page 269) to finish things off. These crab churros are a favorite of mine: the airy batter is a natural complement to the sweet, delicate crab. **MAKES 1¾ pounds (30 doughnuts)**

1 cup whole milk

½ cup unsalted butter

Sea salt

¾ cup plus 2 tablespoons all-purpose flour

5 large eggs, at room temperature

In a medium saucepot bring the milk, butter, and ¾ teaspoon salt to a boil. Add in the flour all at once and stir vigorously with a wooden spoon until the ingredients come together to form a ball. Continue stirring over medium heat until the dough becomes smooth in texture and pulls away from the sides of the pan. Remove from heat.

Transfer the mixture to a stand mixer fitted with the paddle attachment. With the mixer on low speed, slowly add the eggs one at a time, scraping the bowl between every egg. The pâte à choux can be made 1 day in advance and stored in the refrigerator.

Crab Churros with Piquillo Pepper Mayo

These crab churros are a favorite of mine: the airy batter is a natural complement to the sweet, delicate crab. Using pâte à choux instead of a standard doughnut batter also ensures that the crab isn't overcooked; since the dough is already cooked on the stove top, it only needs a few minutes in the fryer to crisp up and warm the churro throughout.

MAKES twenty to thirty 6-inch churros; serves 8 as a snack

PIQUILLO PEPPER MAYO

3 jarred piquillo peppers, well drained and patted dry

Sea salt

½ cup Basic Cider Mayo (page 21)

1 pound jumbo lump crabmeat, carefully checked for shell fragments

Sea salt

Black pepper in a mill

1¾ pounds Pâte à Choux (page 58)

Neutral vegetable oil, for frying

Chop the peppers very finely and season with ⅛ teaspoon salt. Stir into the mayonnaise and store in a lidded container in the refrigerator until ready to serve (the mayo will keep for up to 7 days).

In a large mixing bowl, season the crab with 1½ teaspoons salt and about 6 cranks of pepper and mix well with a rubber spatula. Fold the crab into the pâte à choux batter until the meat is well distributed in the dough. Transfer the batter to a pastry bag fitted with a 1¹⁄₁₆-inch open-star pastry tip.

Line a baking sheet with two or three layers of paper towels. Fill a heavy-bottomed pot or Dutch oven halfway with oil and heat over high heat until the oil reaches 350°F on a deep-fry thermometer.

Working in batches so as not to crowd the churros, pipe 6-inch logs of batter into the hot oil and fry, turning occasionally, until golden brown, about 5 minutes. As the churros are done, transfer them to the paper towel–lined pan and sprinkle with salt. Let the oil come back up to 350°F each time before piping more. Serve hot with the mayo.

Turnip Green Fritters with Whipped Tahini

Turnips have a natural spiciness to them that, when combined with the vegetal nature of the greens and the salty flavor of feta cheese, stands out beautifully against the rich buttery dough. The Mediterranean flavors evoke spanakopita, without having to mess with filo dough. **MAKES 20 to 30 fritters; serves 8 as a snack**

Neutral vegetable oil, for frying

6 ounces turnip greens (from about 3 turnips), washed and thoroughly dried

Sea salt

1 medium turnip (about 3½ ounces)

¾ cup crumbled feta (about 4 ounces)

1¾ pounds Pâte à Choux (page 58)

Whipped Tahini (page 62)

In a large skillet, heat ½ teaspoon oil over medium heat. Add the turnip greens and toss to coat. Add 1 teaspoon water and cover the skillet. Cook for 3 to 4 minutes, until the greens are just wilted and tender. Season lightly with salt, and transfer to a colander. When the greens are cool enough to handle, finely chop, then squeeze the excess water out of the greens. Let the chopped greens sit in a colander over a bowl while you prepare the turnip.

Grate the turnip on the large holes of a box grater. Place the grated turnip in the center of some cheesecloth or a thin dish towel; gather the cloth into a bundle and twist to remove the excess water from the turnip. Empty any water that's drained from the turnip greens from the bowl, then add the greens and the grated turnip to the bowl. Add the feta and toss to combine. Add the choux batter to the bowl and fold until well combined.

Line a baking sheet with two layers of paper towels. Fill a Dutch oven halfway with oil and heat over high heat to 350°F on a kitchen thermometer. Scoop rounded tablespoons of dough into the oil, no more than ten at a time to avoid crowding, and fry until golden brown on all sides, about 5 minutes. Transfer to the prepared baking sheet to drain and sprinkle with salt. Serve hot with the tahini.

note: The fritters can be baked in the oven like *gougères*. Scoop onto a parchment-lined baking sheet into rounds that are 1½ inches in diameter and 1 inch high; bake for 12 minutes in a 400°F convection oven (or a 425°F regular oven); then shut the oven off and let sit in the oven for another 10 minutes. Serve hot.

Whipped Tahini

I've recently developed a bit of a cooking crush on the flavors of the Middle East. There's something so richly satiating, yet light and clean about so many of these dishes. I've never been able to truly unlock their genius, but I'm one step closer thanks to *Olives, Lemons & Za'atar*, a cookbook by Rawia Bishara. In it, I found the secret to one of my favorite condiments, whipped tahini (sesame paste). This recipe is inspired by hers, and is so basic and simple, so endlessly versatile, that I can now imagine it on *everything*, which, to me, is the sign of a great recipe. This tahini makes a beautiful condiment for turnip and feta fritters (see page 61) and adds richness to the roasted carrots (see page 145). I also love it as a dip for crudités. **MAKES about 2½ cups**

1½ cups tahini, well shaken

3 or 4 cloves garlic, crushed and with any green centers removed

1 tablespoon fresh lemon juice

1 teaspoon sea salt

In a food processor, combine the tahini, garlic, lemon juice, and salt and process for 4 to 6 minutes, until the mixture lightens in color. With the motor running, gradually add up to 1 cup water, processing until the mixture is super smooth and creamy, like mayonnaise; the mixture will seize at first before emulsifying into a smooth spread.

Store in a lidded container in the refrigerator for up to 3 days.

Cocktails

Like most people, I love a good cocktail. In addition to delicious ingredients and thoughtful preparations, I love what the cocktail marks . . . be it the end of a long, hard day, the communion of friends, the washing away of heartbreak or sadness, or sometimes, just toasting the setting sun with gratitude for another day. It's a refreshing and simple pause in the wild ride that is modern living, and I'm grateful to have its offerings wrapped up in this craft of cooking and entertaining.

While there's a place for a fancy cocktail, my "Poole's at home" approach to imbibing is fairly straightforward . . . a solid one-and-one (the Greyhound being my standard move), an ice-cold beer-flavored-beer, or a slightly chilled glass of Beaujolais. There's something magical about the cocktail's ability to flip your switch, surrendering the chaos of the day into the backseat. It's a ritual of pleasure, and I love partaking. All things in moderation . . . that said, the cocktail is a harbinger of much appreciated celebration.

Whether you shake or stir (or just crack open a beer), please share the offerings of this chapter with friends. The most important step of each of these recipes is the action of toasting your glasses with the people who hold you to task for a life that is rich and full.

Baked Apple Sangria

3 apples, preferably red, quartered, seeds removed

⅓ cup sugar

1 cinnamon stick, halved

1 whole star anise

3 (2-inch-long) sections orange zest, peeled with a Y-peeler

1 (750-ml) bottle crisp white wine

1 ounce triple sec

1 ounce brandy

1 ounce simple syrup

Dry ginger beer

Sangria is a brilliant way to stretch out a bottle of wine for a crowd, and it taps into my love of collective dishes. Like punch, this is made in a batch and doled out to guests all night long. At Poole's, our sangria changes with the seasons: in the summer, it's blueberries; in the fall, it's scuppernongs. But my favorite version is this winter take, which capitalizes on the beauty of apples and baking spices, while still maintaining a light, bright drinkability. **SERVES 8 to 10**

Preheat a convection oven to 350°F (or a regular oven to 375°F).

Toss the apples in sugar. Transfer to a baking sheet and add the cinnamon stick and star anise. Bake until the apples are golden brown and juicy, about 15 minutes. Remove from the baking sheet and transfer to a container immediately while the juices and sugars are still hot. Add the orange zest and stir. Add the wine, triple sec, brandy, and simple syrup, and cover and refrigerate for 3 days. Strain the mixture, discarding the solids. To serve, add 3 ounces to an ice-filled wine glass and fill to the rim with ginger beer.

Bitter Islander

Like a lot of things in life, I like my tequila simple . . . straight up for sipping, or married with fresh citrus in a well-balanced margarita. This drink bends that rule. It pairs reposado tequila with tea-like hibiscus leaves (think pomegranate fruitiness in a flower) and bitter Campari. The marriage yields a complex smoky bitterness, and bright cocktail without cloying sugar.

Our general manager, Chelley Godwin, dreamt up this cocktail after a trip to her favorite Raleigh taco joint, Taqueria El Toro. **MAKES 1, with extra syrup**

½ ounce fresh lemon juice
½ ounce Campari
1 ounce reposado tequila
1 ounce hibiscus syrup

HIBISCUS SYRUP
½ ounce dried hibiscus
1 cup sugar

To make the hibiscus syrup, in a small saucepan, bring 1 cup water to a boil. Add the hibiscus and remove the water from heat. Let steep for 5 minutes, then stir in the sugar until it dissolves. Strain the liquid, discarding the solids. Store in the refrigerator until ready to use. (The syrup will keep for up to 2 weeks.)

To make the cocktail, combine the lemon juice, Campari, tequila, and syrup in a shaker and fill with ice. Shake until well chilled, then strain into an ice-filled rocks glass.

Garden & Gun Club

This cocktail is a tribute to the beloved publication, the title of which, when read for the first time, always leaves my friends outside of the South a little (adorably) befuddled: "Guns and gardens?" they ask. The magazine is an incredible contribution to the modern South, celebrating and documenting our present culture. I loved it the first time I held a copy in my hands, from its content to the texture of its cover.

One Thanksgiving in my home, years after my father had moved back to New York, a copy of *Garden & Gun* was sitting on an end table in my living room. With the hum of gravy reducing on the stove, and the smell of our family's cornbread dressing wafting through the air, my dad settled into the corner cushion of the couch and killed time with that magazine. He scanned the pages casually, and then he read the whole thing, cover to cover . . . and then again. Though New York was the home he was born into, *Garden & Gun* reminded my father deeply of the South he missed, the South he loved.

Fittingly, this cocktail was designed by Matt Fern, another northern transplant who now proudly calls the South home. Welcome to the club. **MAKES 1**

¾ ounce fresh lemon juice

½ ounce Cointreau

1 ounce dry vermouth

1½ ounces bourbon

3 dashes of orange bitters

1 orange peel strip, for garnish

Combine the lemon juice, Cointreau, vermouth, bourbon, and bitters in a shaker and fill with ice. Shake until well chilled, then strain through a fine-mesh sieve into a chilled martini glass. Garnish with the orange peel.

AC's Greyhound

I don't even really recall when my love for this cocktail began, but I can promise that it is true and pure.

I travel often, and I've enjoyed this drink in airports and hotel bars, and in the restaurants of chef and restaurant friends who know to pour it for me before I even have the chance to order. I've welcomed countless guests into my home with this bright and refreshing drink, and usually refilled their glasses a time or two.

As a true believer that the greatest commodity in this life is time, this drink has become a marker of the importance of pressing pause, rolling our shoulders back, sharing stories, and toasting our glasses. We reference our gatherings as meetings of the Greyhound Society, and we joke that our mission is fighting scurvy. I'm fairly certain we've moved the needle a pinch on the grapefruit market (we prefer Texas grapefruit, for the record). It's nice to have something tangible and delicious that represents your love for your friends and chosen family, and for how important it is to pull each other out of the hustle to do nothing but smile and toast what a remarkable gift friendship is. **MAKES 1**

3 ounces fresh grapefruit juice

3 ounces Tito's vodka

In a tumbler filled with ice, add the grapefruit juice and vodka and stir well to mix.

The "civilian" version: For a less ferocious Greyhound, mix 2 ounces vodka with 4 ounces grapefruit juice.

Milan Mule

I love a Moscow Mule, with its peppery ginger beer and bright notes of lime. I also appreciate it as a great drink to order when you're in foreign territory (a bar where you don't know the experience of the bartender or the vibe of the bar itself).

This version was born during basil season. If you're a regular at Poole's, you've probably noticed a big vase of basil on the bar during the summer. It's delivered to the kitchen door, and after we pull what we need for the day's prep, we carry it up front to be stowed by the bar. Basil, it turns out, keeps best when stored like cut flowers—stems in water, changed frequently, at room temperature. One day, I was standing behind the bar with the bucket of fresh-cut basil in my hands, and Matt Fern was standing on a ladder, updating the chalkboards (we have had so many conversations from these respective positions). The fragrant basil scented our impromptu think tank, and the Milan Mule came to be.

The muddled fresh basil leaves tint the drink with a nearly electric green hue and an undeniable herbal point of reference. In this recipe, we replace the ginger beer with a jalapeño-ginger syrup. The hot pepper and the ginger give a dry heat (a fresh replacement for the ginger beer) and allow us to control its punch. **MAKES 1, with extra syrup**

3 to 4 fresh basil leaves, plus one leaf, for garnish

1 ounce fresh lemon juice

¾ ounce jalapeño-ginger syrup

1½ ounces Tito's vodka

JALAPEÑO-GINGER SYRUP

3 ounces fresh ginger, peeled, and roughly chopped

1 ounce jalapeños, stems and half the seeds removed, sliced

1¼ cups sugar

To make the syrup, combine the ginger, jalapeños, sugar, and 1¼ cups water in a medium saucepan. Bring to a boil, then lower the heat and simmer, stirring occasionally for 30 minutes. Remove from the heat and let sit for 30 more minutes, then strain through a fine-mesh sieve, discarding the solids. Let cool completely before using. (The syrup will keep in an airtight container in the refrigerator up to 1 week.)

To make the cocktail, put the basil in the bottom of a shaking tin and gently muddle with a muddler (or, in a pinch, the back of a wooden spoon). Add the lemon juice, syrup, and vodka, fill the shaker with ice, and shake until well chilled. Strain through a fine-mesh sieve into an ice-filled highball glass and garnish with an additional basil leaf.

Wake County Cooler

I literally took my first steps as a toddler toward a glass of iced tea. I looked up from my seated baby stance on the carpet, made eye contact with the sweating glass held by a family friend across the room, and took flight. Three steps got me there, and I grabbed the prize with both hands, bathing myself and the carpet in the majority of the spoils. My taste for the stuff was solidified from that moment.

Iced tea is plentiful here in the South, almost always dealt in "bottomless" glasses, and usually sweet. I've tried to curb my consumption, but when I can't fight the urge, I take my iced tea "half-cut" (half sweetened/half unsweetened). At Poole's however, the only iced tea we have is in the form of a cocktail we call the Wake County Cooler (we have borne witness to more than our share of griping over this decision, as Southerners LOVE their iced tea). As a tribute to our county, Wake, it also celebrates "half-cut" sweetness status.

There are lots of tea-infused vodkas on the market, but we prefer to infuse our own, so we can control the sweetness of the drink, the quality of the black tea, and the vodka of our choice (Tito's is my preference). If you like your cocktails on the dry side, leave out or limit the simple syrup added in at the mixing of the drink. **MAKES 1, with extra infused vodka**

½ ounce fresh lemon juice

½ ounce simple syrup

1½ ounces black tea vodka

Soda, as needed

1 lemon wedge, for garnish

BLACK TEA VODKA

1 ounce loose black tea

1 (750-ml) bottle Tito's vodka

To make the black tea vodka, add the tea to the vodka and steep for 3 hours. Strain through a fine-mesh sieve and store the vodka in the refrigerator until ready to use. (The infused vodka will keep in the refrigerator for up to 6 months.)

To make the cocktail, combine the lemon juice, simple syrup, and vodka in a shaker and fill with ice. Shake until well chilled, then strain into an ice-filled highball glass. Top to the rim with soda and garnish with a lemon wedge.

The Captain's G & T

My appreciation for the Gin and Tonic came from my long-time best friend Julie's husband, Brooks Hagan. Brooks is a really together type of person. He's a textile professor at RISD and one of the brightest design minds in the country. With the mission of greatness on his shoulders (he's sculpting young minds after all) he's wound tight in the best way. (I must also mention, he's the father of my beautiful godson, Asa.)

While Brooks and Julie lived in Brooklyn (and before Asa), I'd visit frequently, and after a long day, Brooks generally would make the team a round of cocktails—almost always G & Ts. It wasn't a drink that I would voluntarily order, but Brooks's G & T was different. Packed with lime wedges and extra bubbly tonic, I loved the drink and the time spent with friends, and I even enjoyed swallowing my own words about not being a G & T drinker.

As we threw a couple back, the focused and appropriately wound Brooks would visibly loosen up and look to Jules and me with the question, "Alright, what are we getting into tonight? We could probably go out for a few more drinks, right?" Jules would lean over and whisper through a smile . . . "Captain Just One More has arrived."

And so, this is The Captain's G & T. I hope it helps you take that edge off and find your inner captain. **MAKES 1**

½ lime, cut into 4 wedges

2 ounces London dry gin
(Brooks likes Beefeater)

5 to 6 ounces high-quality
tonic water

Squeeze the lime wedges over a Collins glass, then drop the juiced wedges into the glass. Fill the glass with ice, then add the gin and tonic water. Stir with a long spoon to mix.

Beer Can Michelada

The Michelada is a drink that always appealed to me more in theory than in reality. Though I am passionate about beer-flavored-beer, I'm just not a beer over ice kind of gal. My pal Karin Stanley righted my ship on the spicy classic, utilizing the can itself as the serving vessel. A christening swig of beer clears the perfect amount of room in the can for all of the spice, citrus, and umami you'll add to take this beverage to new heights. It's an excellent brunch drink, and also it's perfect for an outdoor hang. **SERVES 10**

½ cup fresh lime juice

½ cup Worcestershire

1 teaspoon Cholula hot sauce

1 teaspoon Tabasco

10 (12-ounce) cans mildly flavored beer (such as Modelo or Stroh's)

Kosher salt

Black pepper in a mill

note: Feel free to add more hot sauce to your mix to increase the heat.

In a squeeze bottle or pitcher, combine the lime juice, Worcestershire, and hot sauces. To serve, drink a big gulp from one of the cans of beer, then add ¾ ounce of the lime juice mixture to the can. Sprinkle some salt and pepper on the rim of the can and serve.

| BEER-FLAVORED BEER |

I have so much respect for all of our talented pals making delicious craft beer here and all over the country. These products are deliciously complex and creative on a whole new level. That said, sometimes, I'm just in the mood for a beer-flavored beer. Ice-cold, simple, refreshing. I'm talking about the kind of beer you want someone to slide down the bar to you when you sit down after a long day in the sun. The kind of beer that is implied when Homer Simpson avoids going home to Marge and the kids, and instead, parks it at Moe's Tavern, throwing back foam-capped mugs of Duff. Beer. Flavored. Beer.

On the hunt for the right selection for Poole's Diner, Matt Fern and I floated ideas for something that people didn't see at every single bar in our city. We wanted something delicious at an entry-level pricepoint, an alternative to PBR and High Life that we could build a following around. Fern smiled and said, "What about Stroh's?" The last time I'd had a Stroh's, I wasn't even of legal drinking age. We were both high on the idea, so Fern hit the pavement to find the distributor. It turned out that the company who held the distribution rights to Stroh's also distributed PBR, and chose not to sell the Stroh's. This made Stroh's an essentially dead brand. As you can imagine, this only fueled our obsession. Fern found a little gas station in Fayetteville, North Carolina (an hour from Raleigh) that held distribution rights for that county. So, we of course did the only reasonable thing we could imagine: once a month we rented a U-Haul van, drove to Fayetteville, and packed up as many cases as we could haul. It was a matter of principle—delicious beer-flavored principle.

Vinaigrettes

At Poole's, we call our salads "vinaigrettes." We do this because it breaks salad out of its pigeonholed place on the menu and because vinaigrette is arguably the most important part of these dishes. It's also the characteristic they all share.

First, let's dispel the idea that salad is defined by lettuce. In the South, salad frequently refers to a dish bound with mayonnaise; in the Midwest, the meaning of the word is looser and can include dishes dressed in Cool Whip or cream cheese (look up "Snickers salad"—yes, it's a real thing).

My definition is even less rigid: in my kitchen, "salad" is any presentation of a few ingredients, at least one of them from the garden, united by acid. In fact, acid is the most crucial element of a salad's success. Instead of taking the lead, it pushes the ingredients forward, like the cheerleader at the base of the pyramid. And vinaigrette, an acidic sauce of vinegar and oil, is salad's team captain. It's what holds everything together, and it balances the two things that make food taste great: fat and acid.

If you let it be, salad is nimble and inspires confidence. It can house a variety of textures, flavors, and temperatures, and it's a chameleon, fitting beautifully into any stage or style of a meal. We're used to eating our salads at the beginning of a meal and with good reason: cold salads buy time while hot dishes finish cooking, and the acid in many salads primes our palate for the rich flavors that usually come later in a meal.

I prefer having my salad alongside the rest of the meal, where it can help cut the richness and round out the flavors of meat or fish. Think of a rich braised pork shank nestled alongside the bright kick of a vinaigrette-coated sweet potato and poblano pepper salad. That said, I always conceptualize the salads we offer at Poole's as dishes that can stand on their own rather than as accompaniments or precursors to something else.

Since there are so many roads to a delicious salad, it can be hard to know where to begin. So I start with this set of guidelines to determine whether certain components will work together in a salad:

- Do these ingredients share a season and are they local?

- If not, is the combination delicious enough that I can bend my commitment to working with an ingredient that I've pulled from another climate or season? Sometimes, for the sake of a dish's awesomeness, the answer is yes.

- Have I created a variety of textures? Do creamy or soft ingredients have a crispy or crunchy counterpoint?

- Does the acid in my vinaigrette complement the other ingredients? For example, cider vinegar is a natural with other flavors of autumn, such as apples or brussels sprouts, while tomatoes, which have natural sugars and acid, do well with brighter, lighter vinegars, such as champagne or white balsamic.

- Is it delicious?

Beyond that, anything goes. At Poole's, any of the dishes in the Vinaigrettes section of the menu can be eaten together or can complement a dish from any of the other savory sections of the menu.

So, let's get to know our head cheerleader a little better. Vinaigrette is a sauce made by emulsifying oil and vinegar, and the first time I successfully made it was the moment I really felt I had a true understanding of cooking. Since then, I've made countless batches, but I've never lost my romantic fascination with the simple technique. Unlike a squeeze of lemon juice or a drizzle of straight vinegar, a vinaigrette brings an undeniable roundness and balance to whatever it touches.

Learning from Vinaigrette

I'm a sensory learner. Most recipes are written as formulas and measurements, but they become much more useful to me when I can combine them with an image of the colors and textures of the dish, hear the sounds and rhythms of the kitchen, and smell the fragrance of an ingredient as it changes form.

Vinaigrette is one of those instantly gratifying processes in the kitchen where the ingredients change before your eyes (and ears and mouth), morphing from two immiscible properties to a single, seamless entity. The transformation offers plenty of sensory cues for the home cook, so it's the perfect introduction to cooking based on feel rather than rote instruction.

Read the cues. Make one of the vinaigrettes by following the recipe, paying attention to the changes in appearance and sound (yes, sound!) as you go (start with the Red Wine Vinaigrette on page 84). Then attempt to make a vinaigrette without referring to the measurements, going simply by feel. If you're paying attention, you'll be able to produce a stellar vinaigrette without ever glancing at a recipe.

Use a binding agent. In almost every vinaigrette I make, there's a scant amount of Dijon mustard. While this is partially for taste, it's mostly to help keep the vinaigrette stable. Mustard is a binding agent, like a pair of handcuffs that holds together the opposing forces of oil and vinegar. (Egg yolks and honey also work great as binding agents.) If you leave it out, your vinaigrette will separate quickly. (There's a time and a place for a broken vinaigrette, but the key is being able to control that effect to your desire.)

VINAIGRETTE STORAGE

You'll notice that many of the vinaigrette recipes in this chapter make more than you'll need for just one salad. This is intentional. Many of these vinaigrettes have elements that don't adapt well to a yield of just a few tablespoons, so you have to make them in larger batches. But more than that, most basic vinaigrettes will keep in your refrigerator for about 2 weeks because they're made of preservation-enhancing ingredients: vinegar and fat. These two rockstars will keep any fresh ingredients (like shallots or citrus) from turning. Since vinaigrettes have endless applications, it only makes sense that you'd want some extra to keep around, right? Please note that there's an exception here: any dressing with eggs or dairy has a shorter lifespan (3 to 4 days in the refrigerator).

Red Wine Vinaigrette

One of the most important sauces in the Poole's kitchen is the red wine vinaigrette that we make for our Bibb Lettuce Salad (page 87). It's as simple as it sounds. There are no tricks or fancy ingredients—just good red wine vinegar, neutral vegetable oil, shallots, mustard, and salt and pepper. It thrills me to no end that something this basic could be so magical, and it should thrill you too. It'll take you five minutes to make this recipe, but having a stash of it in the fridge is like having a blank check. Fresh greens, a grain salad, delicate seafood, a roasted sweet potato—all will be improved by a tablespoon of this stuff drizzled over the top.

I've written this recipe with way more detail and observations than you'll see in most recipes. There are measurements, but the real takeaway is noticing the stages of change. If you can hold on to those, you can make a vinaigrette without a recipe, and that opens up endless opportunities. **MAKES about 1⅓ cups**

1 tablespoon minced shallots
⅓ cup red wine vinegar
1½ teaspoons Dijon mustard
Sea salt
1 cup neutral vegetable oil

In a mixing bowl, cover the shallots with the vinegar. Let marinate for 15 minutes. This allows the shallots to bleed flavor directly into the vinegar (which is more potent before the oil is added) and to soak up some of the vinegar so they will pack a sharp pickle-like punch even after the oil is added. Taste a bit of raw shallot, then taste a bit after it has marinated: that aggressive oniony heat will have mellowed into an astringent snap.

Using a whisk, stir the mustard and a pinch of salt into the shallot and vinegar mixture. Be sure the mustard is totally incorporated into the vinegar, as it needs to be fully incorporated in order to do its job as binding agent.

Put the oil into a measuring cup with a pouring spout. Begin whisking the vinegar mixture in a circular motion. (I place a damp towel under the mixing bowl to keep the bowl from spinning as I whisk.) Slowly drizzle the oil into the vinegar mixture in a thin, steady stream, aiming it at the side of the bowl so that it is taken up into the current of the vinegar whirlpool; avoiding pouring directly into the center of the bowl, as there is not as much vinegar there and the oil will be less likely to emulsify. Whisk continuously until all of the oil is added to the bowl. I know that I'm close.

when I see the whisk begin to leave subtle trails in the mixture, and I hear the sound of the liquid circling the bowl turn a bit deeper and fuller. These cues suggest that the mixture is binding and thickening. The color will turn from a deep maroon-pink into a softer pastel that's just barely blush colored.

Using a spoon, taste the vinaigrette for salt and season to your preference. I like to under-season at this point: it makes the vinaigrette more versatile for pairing with other ingredients that may have varying salt levels. Black or white pepper are natural complements to basic vinaigrette, but I prefer adding pepper later, if the flavors call for it when I'm incorporating the vinaigrette into a dish. This way it's also fresher and more vibrant, and I can adjust the grind to the tune of the other ingredients. As a friend of mine says, "You can't put the toothpaste back in the tube"—we can always add something, but we can't always take it back, especially when it comes to salt and pepper.

| VARIATIONS |

For White Balsamic Vinaigrette, swap out the red wine vinegar for white balsamic vinegar and add 1$^{1}/_{2}$ teaspoons honey along with the mustard.

For White Balsamic–Thyme Vinaigrette, swap out the red wine vinegar for white balsamic vinegar, add 1 tablespoon minced fresh thyme to the shallots and 1$^{1}/_{2}$ teaspoons honey to the mustard.

For Sweet Onion Vinaigrette, swap out the red wine vinegar for champagne vinegar, and swap out the shallots for 3 tablespoons minced Vidalia onions. Add 2 teaspoons honey and omit the mustard.

For Banyuls Vinaigrette, swap out the red wine vinegar for Banyuls vinegar and add 1$^{1}/_{2}$ teaspoons honey with the mustard.

Bibb Lettuce Salad

From day one at Poole's Diner, this dish has stayed exactly the same, even as we matured around it. For all of the classic dishes we've pulled apart and reinvented in the name of a new approach to comfort food, this is one we couldn't bring ourselves to touch.

In the kitchen, we call this "Eliza's salad," for Eliza Kraft Olander. She is my hero and one of my best friends, and she just happens to love this salad. After she requested some of the vinaigrette to take home one night, we made it a rule that the salad station would always keep an extra pint prepped in case she made an appearance.

Use the freshest Bibb lettuce you can get your hands on—I like to use a mix of red and green. We stack the leaves into a tall pile, not for any kind of fussy presentation, but for utility: by doing so, the leaves function like cups, catching some of the sharp, briny Parmesan that is shaved generously over the top. Please don't be shy with your shaving when you're making this at home: it should look like it's snowed all over the plate. **SERVES 4**

Leaves from 2 heads Bibb lettuce, washed and thoroughly dried

1 teaspoon sea salt

Black pepper in a mill

½ cup Red Wine Vinaigrette (page 84)

8 ounces Parmigiano-Reggiano (I like Vacche Rosse)

Combine the lettuce leaves, salt, and 30 cranks of the pepper mill in a large bowl. Mix with your hands to distribute the salt and pepper. Add the vinaigrette and fold gently with your hands until the vinaigrette has coated each leaf. Divide the leaves among four plates, stacking the leaves on top of one another to make a tall pile. Finely grate 2 ounces of the cheese over each salad; it will seem like a lot of cheese, and that is just right.

Arugula with Button Mushrooms, Crispy Sopressata, and Sherry-Sherry Vinaigrette

This salad was inspired by a dish I fell hard for at my favorite New Orleans restaurant, Cochon. My pal, chef Stephen Stryjewski, does a gorgeous job of marrying the food traditions of Cajun country with the evolving energy of a modern New Orleans. His dish combined deep-fried beef jerky (you could stop right there and I wouldn't complain) with perfectly acidic bits of grilled lemon and velvety slices of cremini mushroom.

In my version, I swap the beef jerky for oven-crisped sopressata (which also makes an excellent stand-in for bacon in a BLT) and lighten it up with a handful of peppery arugula. But I don't change a thing about the mushrooms, which are a tender reminder of the classic salad bars I love. We use a robust Asiago-like cheese called Calvander from Chapel Hill Creamery; if you can't get it, a good Asiago is what you want.

The double "sherry" in the recipe's name isn't a typo. The vinaigrette that binds this salad gets its flavor from sherry in two styles: sherry vinegar and PX (or Pedro Ximénez) sherry, a sweet, dark, fortified version of the wine. The vinaigrette requires a few steps, but it is truly worth it, and this recipe makes more than you'll need for the salad. Use the extra to baste grilled fish or shrimp or as a dressing for an avocado and crab salad. **SERVES 4, with extra vinaigrette**

SHERRY-SHERRY VINAIGRETTE

1 cup unsalted butter, cut into chunks

½ Meyer lemon (if you can't find a Meyer lemon, use a regular lemon)

Sea salt

2 tablespoons minced shallots

⅓ cup sherry vinegar

⅓ cup PX sherry

1 teaspoon Dijon mustard

1½ teaspoons honey

1 cup neutral vegetable oil

Continued

To make the vinaigrette, place the butter in a small saucepan over medium heat. Melt the butter; when it stops foaming, watch it carefully, swirling the pan occasionally. The butter will begin to darken in color and smell toasty; remove it from the heat when it reaches a golden honey color, about 3 minutes after it stops foaming. Strain the butter through a fine-mesh sieve into a small bowl and set aside.

Slice the lemon paper-thin on a mandoline and pick out any seeds. Season the lemon slices lightly with sea salt. Heat a cast-iron skillet over medium-high heat and use a paper towel and tongs to wipe down the interior of the pan with a thin layer of neutral vegetable oil. Add the lemon slices in a single layer; char on one side for about 2 minutes. Transfer to a cutting board and let cool completely.

Mince the charred lemons and add them to a mixing bowl with the shallots, sherry vinegar, and PX sherry. Let marinate for 15 minutes.

12 thin slices sopressata
(about 4 ounces total)

12 ounces arugula

8 cremini or button mushrooms,
sliced paper thin

2 small red onions, sliced paper thin

Black pepper in a mill

8 ounces robust Asiago

Whisk in the mustard and honey until fully incorporated. While whisking, slowly drizzle in the brown butter, then the vegetable oil, until the mixture is completely emulsified. Season with salt to taste. The vinaigrette can be made up to 5 days in advance and stored in a lidded container in the refrigerator.

To make the salad, preheat a convection oven to 325°F (or a regular oven to 350°F). Line a baking sheet with a layer of parchment. Arrange the sopressata in a single layer (so the slices do not overlap) on the lined baking sheet. Place a second piece of parchment over the sopressata and lay a second baking sheet on top to weigh the sopressata down (this will keep it from curling in the oven). Bake until super crispy, about 7 minutes. Remove from the oven and let cool.

In a bowl, combine the arugula, mushrooms, onions, and 8 cranks of the pepper mill and toss lightly with your hands. Break up the crispy sopressata in your hands and sprinkle over the salad. Add 6 tablespoons of the vinaigrette and toss to coat. Grate the cheese over the top of the salad, toss to distribute, and serve.

note: This recipe features mutiple salt-forward ingredients, so I haven't included salt as a necessary component. That said, if you feel like the dish requires additional salt, I encourage you to season to taste.

Charred Onions

There has never been a grill at Poole's, so we've looked for creative ways to channel the energy and reward of live fire through our stove top. Charred onions are one of the simplest and most straightforward ways to do that. It also lets us utilize the flavor of the onion, while muting some of the unpredictable "hotness" that certain alliums can carry (and haunt us with the morning after). Additionally, onions, in particular, take well to the process of charring, because they have a good amount of natural sugar, which chars quickly in the presence of a hot surface (cast-iron skillets are ideal for this). Like a little more crunch and fire in your onion? Then leave one side of the onion completely raw.

You'll find charred onions used in a number of places in this book, but I've placed them here so you can pull them into your cooking beyond these recipes. Throw a handful on top of game day nachos, or add a few spoons of them into a quinoa salad. I like them in potato salad, and mixed into other charred and marinated vegetables.

Rain or shine, the backyard barbecue is now in your back pocket.

MAKES 1 cup diced charred onions

1 red onion
Sea salt

Place a cast-iron skillet over medium-high heat, and use a paper towel and tongs to rub the interior of the pan with a thin layer of neutral vegetable oil. Slice the red onion across the equator into half-inch-thick slabs. Season both sides of each slab of onion generously with sea salt, and place the broadest side down in the preheated cast iron. Cook until the face of the onion is charred, about 5 to 6 minutes. Flip the slab over and cook 3 to 4 minutes more. Remove the onions from the pan and let them rest with the charred side up. Once they cool to room temperature, slice each slab of onion from top to bottom, and then from left to right (imagine a tic-tac-toe grid) in ½-inch squares.

(If charring the onion in advance, keep the slabs intact. The onion slabs will keep for 3 to 4 days in the refrigerator. Dice or slice when ready to use.)

Mustard Frills with Crispy Okra, Charred Onions, and Tahini Dressing

This salad incorporates a few simple but potent techniques that can and should be used beyond this application. The crispy okra was inspired by my pal Vish Bhatt, chef of the Snack Bar in Oxford, Mississippi. He uses it in the summer edition of his Indian-inspired bistro menu. Since you're going to the trouble of deep-frying, I suggest making more than the recipe calls for; eat the leftover okra as a snack with leftover Tahini Dressing.

Now, about that dressing. I moved to Raleigh at age eighteen to attend North Carolina State University, and one of my first discoveries was the Rathskeller, a bar planted in the middle of the campus-adjacent main drag of Hillsborough Street. Sage friends who referred to themselves as "Olde Raleigh" showed me how to battle my hangovers with the magical combination of Monterey cheese fries (steak fries covered in melted Monterey Jack cheese and roasted green chiles) and a soup cup–size side of the most craveable tahini dressing you could ever dream up.

Years after my first dose, I managed to coax the recipe for the dressing out of a certain Raleigh legend who occasionally made a little cash as a prep cook at the Rathskeller. I took a blood oath that night never to tell how (and from whom) I unlocked the mystery of the recipe.

The Rathskeller, like many great places in many great cities, has since closed its doors. My interpretation of its tahini dressing recipe has for a long time felt like one of my most prized possessions. But I'd quickly give it up for the chance to walk back into that weird little landmark and order those hangover-damning fries and that mysteriously curative dressing.

For this salad, cut the okra as thinly as possible—with a mandoline if you have one. Red mustard frills are a spicy variety of mustard greens with frilly leaves; if you can't find it, mizuna or curly kale would also work here. The Tahini Dressing makes 4 cups (you need just ½ cup for the recipe); it seems like a lot, but you'll be so grateful to have extra of this dressing hanging out in your fridge (it will keep for 7 days). Use it as a dipping sauce for crudités or pour it over French fries, Rathskeller-style. **SERVES 4, with extra dressing**

TAHINI DRESSING

3 tablespoons diced green
    bell pepper

½ cup diced yellow onion

1 clove garlic

½ cup fresh lemon juice

4 teaspoons lemon zest

6 tablespoons soy sauce

1½ teaspoons freshly ground
    black pepper

1 tablespoon Dijon mustard

1 cup tahini

1 cup plus 2 tablespoons
    neutral vegetable oil

⅓ cup toasted sesame oil

Neutral vegetable oil, for frying

8 okra pods, stemmed and
    thinly sliced lengthwise

Sea salt

1 cup diced Charred Onion
    (page 91)

12 ounces red mustard frills,
    leaves torn and tender
    stems roughly chopped

Black pepper in a mill

¼ cup Red Wine Vinaigrette
    (page 84)

To make the dressing, combine the green pepper, onion, garlic, lemon juice and zest, soy sauce, black pepper, mustard, and 3 tablespoons water in a food processor and blend on low until the mixture forms a puree. Add the tahini and blend on high speed until well combined. With the motor running, drizzle in the vegetable oil, followed by the sesame oil. Taste and adjust the seasoning if necessary. Pour into a lidded container and store in the refrigerator until ready to use.

Line a plate with two or three layers of paper towel. Pour 2 inches of oil into a heavy-bottomed pot over high heat until it reaches 325°F on a deep-fry thermometer.

Add the okra slices to the oil and fry until they are a deep golden brown, about 1½ minutes, then agitating slightly while they cook to keep them from sticking together. Transfer to a paper towel–lined plate and sprinkle with salt.

In a large mixing bowl, combine the mustard frills, onion, ½ teaspoon salt, 10 cranks of the pepper mill, and the vinaigrette and toss until fully incorporated. Season with salt to taste.

Pour ½ cup of the tahini dressing in a pool in the center of a platter and pile the salad on top, garnishing with the okra pods. Make sure to drag the salad through the tahini dressing as you serve to get all of the flavors.

Charred Brussels Sprouts with Pomegranate, Pecorino, and White Balsamic Vinaigrette

This elegant salad would be right at home as part of a fancy dinner party, but it also channels something far more utilitarian: coleslaw. Thinly sliced brussels sprouts have the intense heartiness of cabbage, with an even stronger vegetal funk delivered in its tiny package. Charring them in a cast-iron skillet helps tame that note, while still delivering crispy cabbage-like bite.

I love to use pomegranate seeds in salads in lieu of nuts. They offer that same crunchy texture while also providing a subtle spike of sweet and sour. Plus, with the abundance of nut allergies floating around these days, pomegranate is a great sub-in. I've also made this salad with the addition of sliced pear, which is a delicious alternative. While regular balsamic vinegar can overpower, white balsamic is expertly suited to take this salad to new heights. **SERVES 6 to 8, or 4 as a main course**

8 ounces brussels sprouts

Sea salt

4 ounces hearty mixed lettuces, torn

½ cup pomegranate seeds (from about ½ pomegranate)

½ cup thinly sliced red onion (from about ¼ large onion)

4 ounces Pecorino

½ cup White Balsamic Vinaigrette (page 85)

Black pepper in a mill

Heat a cast-iron skillet over medium-high heat. Use a paper towel and tongs to rub the interior of the pan with a thin layer of neutral vegetable oil.

Trim any sprouts with dark stems, taking care to trim only the very tips (you need the stems intact to keep the brussels sprouts together). Thinly slice the sprouts lengthwise. Add a handful of the sprouts to the pan and let them char on one side, about 2 minutes; stir the sprouts for a minute more, then transfer to a baking sheet and season with salt. Repeat with the remaining sprouts.

In a large bowl, combine the charred sprouts, lettuce, pomegranate seeds, and red onion. Shave the Pecorino into strips with a Y-peeler and set aside.

Drizzle the sprout mixture with the vinaigrette and toss with your hands to coat. Add the Pecorino, breaking the strips up into small pieces with your hands. Toss again. Season to taste with freshly ground black pepper and salt if desired; usually I omit additional salt, since the cheese is so salty, but I go heavy on the black pepper, using up to 8 cranks.

Summer Melon with Country Ham, Burrata, Toasted Chiles, and White Balsamic Vinaigrette

Country ham is a cherished ingredient in the South, but I didn't eat it growing up. The diners and greasy spoons always served it cut into thick slices and bathed in red-eye gravy, a presentation that didn't appeal to my sensitive young palate.

The first time I had prosciutto, however, it arrived in nearly see-through slices, so paper-thin that you could imagine them, if dropped from above, floating from left to right like feathers. Later, as country ham came into fashion as an artisanal ingredient, chefs began to honor it with the same precise knife treatment, allowing the nuances to sing more clearly and its flavors to be enjoyed more thoughtfully. The South's country ham found refinement not by changing its nature but by shifting its presentation. I grew to love it through these delicate thin slices, but I matured into loving those thick slices, too.

This dish updates the old idea of thick spears of melon complemented by thin slices of prosciutto. Here, the melon is thinly sliced so the ingredients are equally matched in every bite.

You have a few options for serving this dish: arrange all the different components on individual plates, or create one large Pollock-like platter. I like using both cantaloupe and honeydew melons, though you'll only need about a quarter of a small melon in total. Just save the rest for another use (like breakfast!).

Ground Aleppo pepper, which has a distinct fruitiness, is what I use for chile flakes here, but any will work. If you can't find burrata, you could substitute fresh mozzarella or any mild creamy cheese. **SERVES 4 to 6**

1 teaspoon dried chile flakes

⅛ small cantaloupe

⅛ small honeydew

4 ounces very thinly sliced country ham

8 ounces burrata

Black pepper in a mill

¼ cup White Balsamic Vinaigrette (page 85)

Place the chile flakes in a small skillet and set over medium heat. Toast for about 90 seconds, stirring frequently. Remove from the heat and let cool completely; set aside while you prepare the salad.

Peel and remove the seeds from each piece of melon and use a mandoline or Y-peeler to cut the flesh into thin ribbons. Layer the melon slices and country ham slices on a large platter. Tear the burrata balls into pieces and scatter them over the surface of the ham and melon. Sprinkle the chile flakes over the top and season with 8 cranks of the pepper mill. Finish the dish by drizzling the vinaigrette over the top.

Tomatoes with Grilled Cornbread and White Balsamic–Thyme Vinaigrette

The best part of a ripe tomato is the natural *jus* that a few pinches of salt can coax out of it. This was surely what inspired Tuscans to create the *panzanella* salad, that classic dish of tomatoes, day-old country bread, and olive oil. Here, grilled skillet cornbread stands in for rustic country bread; it sponges up the tomato's juices while still holding its form and texture. Plus, I promise that you can master rock-star cornbread in almost any climate or oven, which is not always true for rustic country loaves. You'll find an easy, seriously delicious cornbread recipe on page 100.

In addition to the cornbread, I've also twisted this salad in the direction of one of my favorite components of the American steakhouse experience—the wedge salad—with the addition of blue cheese and red onions. **SERVES 4**

2 tablespoons unsalted butter

4 wedges Cornbread (page 100), each ¹⁄₁₂ of a skillet

4 small heirloom tomatoes, cored

1 teaspoon sea salt

Black pepper in a mill

¼ red onion, thinly sliced

½ cup White Balsamic–Thyme Vinaigrette (page 85)

4 ounces creamy blue cheese

In a skillet over medium-high heat, melt the butter. Place the cornbread cut side down in the pan and cook until it's a deep golden brown; flip and repeat on the other side. Transfer to a plate and reserve.

Cut the tomatoes into wedges and place in a mixing bowl. Season with the salt and 15 cranks of the pepper mill. Add the red onion and vinaigrette and mix well.

To serve, place the cornbread slices in the center of a platter and arrange the tomato mixture around it. Crumble the blue cheese over the top and serve. (You can also plate this salad individually, placing 1 slice of cornbread on each plate and dividing the tomato mixture and cheese among the plates.)

Cornbread

Cornbread is one of my major go-to ingredients. I grew up on skillet-baked cornbread, and I still love to snack on a wedge with a rub of cold butter. But as wonderful as it is in its pure state, I think I've come to love cornbread even more as an ingredient. In this book, you'll find it binding crab cakes (see page 225), griddled to a state of crouton-ness as the centerpiece of an updated *panzanella* (see page 99), and crumbled to add a sweet and nutty crunch to baked oysters (see page 57). It's supplanted basic bread crumbs for me.

Cornbread, unlike yeasted wheat breads, comes together in a flash. I usually make two loaves at a time and freeze one for a rainy day (or for anytime I'm in need of some textural heft). To freeze, let the cornbread cool completely and wrap it in two tight layers of plastic wrap. To thaw, let it sit at room temperature overnight. **MAKES one 12-inch skillet bread or 16 cups (50 ounces) crumbs**

6 large eggs, beaten

2½ cups buttermilk

¾ cup unsalted butter, melted and cooled, plus 1 tablespoon cold unsalted butter

2½ cups coarsely ground cornmeal

1½ cups corn flour or finely ground cornmeal

1 tablespoon plus 2 teaspoons baking powder

1 tablespoon fine sea salt

Preheat a convection oven to 375°F (or a regular oven to 400°F); place a 12-inch cast-iron skillet in the oven to heat.

In a large bowl, combine the eggs, buttermilk, and melted butter. In a second large bowl, combine the cornmeal, corn flour, baking powder, and salt. Add the wet ingredients to the dry and fold with a rubber spatula to combine.

Pull the hot skillet from the oven. Add the 1 tablespoon cold butter to the pan and swirl to melt, coating the bottom and sides of the pan. Pour the batter into the hot buttered skillet. Return the skillet to the oven, and bake for 25 to 30 minutes, until set. Flip the cornbread out onto a cooling rack.

Serve warm, or let cool completely for later use or freezing. For cornbread crumbs, cut the loaf into wedges and pulse in the food processor. Store in a resealable plastic bag in the refrigerator for 1 week (or the freezer for up to 1 month).

Tomato Season(ing)

Tomatoes just may be my spirit animal. They are certainly one of my favorite ingredients, and are frequently my answer to the question "What does this dish need?" It's a relationship that started early for me: my father grew tomato plants each year, and we ate fresh tomatoes with a spoonful of mayonnaise as part of dinner almost every night of tomato season. Tomatoes were as much a totem of childhood summers as the absence of homework or the trips to the beach.

From June to the last dying whispers of warm weather in early October, Poole's has an heirloom tomato salad on the menu. North Carolina has a climate that tomatoes seem to love, and we have no shortage of gorgeous options to choose from, including favorites like Green Zebra, Cherokee Purple, and German Johnson.

The best part of a great tomato is that it needs very little to shine as the centerpiece of a meal. My favorite raw tomato dishes are almost embarrassingly simple, but there is one easy step that takes them from great to out of this world: bleeding. It sounds medieval, but it translates to something harmless: season your ripe, sliced tomatoes with generous sprinkles of sea salt and freshly ground black pepper and let them sit for a few minutes (I think 7 minutes is the magic number). The tomatoes quickly start to let go of some of their juices (hence, bleeding), and the sugars intensify to make the tomato taste especially rich, ripe, and wonderful. This step is crucial for tomato salads, as well as for the classically Southern tomato sandwich (which must be made, in my opinion, on regular white bread with Duke's mayonnaise).

Heirloom Tomatoes with Crushed Olives, Crispy Quinoa, and White Anchovy Dressing

I could profess my love for heirloom tomatoes over and over again, but in this case, the other elements of this dish are strong enough to carry even a mediocre tomato to a new level of deliciousness.

The fried quinoa is also featured in our tuna tartare (see page 48). When I take the time to cook something like this at home, I try to find as many different ways to use it as possible. One of these head-scratching sessions led to this salad, and now it's a house favorite.

The creamy white anchovy vinaigrette is a love note to Caesar salad (it'll make more than you need—enough to make this salad twice; keep it in the fridge for 3 to 4 days). Who doesn't love a perfect Caesar salad? I may just start finishing my Caesar salads with crispy quinoa instead of starchy croutons. **SERVES 4, with extra dressing**

WHITE ANCHOVY DRESSING

Zest of 1 lemon

2 tablespoons champagne vinegar

1 large egg yolk

½ teaspoon sea salt

1¼ teaspoons Dijon mustard

1 clove garlic, roughly chopped

1½ white anchovies, roughly chopped

1 tablespoon Worcestershire

½ cup neutral vegetable oil

¼ cup olive oil

4 medium heirloom tomatoes, cored and sliced ½ inch thick

Sea salt

Black pepper in a mill

½ cup torn fresh parsley leaves

6 chives, cut into ½-inch-long pieces (about 1 tablespoon)

¼ cup Crispy Quinoa (page 48)

½ cup crushed, pitted Castelvetrano olives

Zest of 1 lemon

2 tablespoons olive oil

To make the dressing, place the lemon zest in a container and cover with the vinegar. Let marinate for 10 minutes.

In food processor, puree the egg yolk, salt, mustard, garlic, and anchovies.

With the machine running, drizzle in the vinegar–lemon zest mixture, and then the Worcestershire sauce. Puree for 1 minute, incorporating air, which helps make it creamy.

Slowly drizzle in the vegetable oil, followed by the olive oil. Transfer to a lidded container and store in the refrigerator until ready to use.

Place the tomato slices on a wire rack set over a baking sheet and dust the cut surfaces with sea salt and freshly ground black pepper. Let sit for 10 minutes.

Meanwhile, in a medium bowl, combine the parsley, chives, quinoa, olives, and lemon zest. Toss to combine, then drizzle with the olive oil and any tomato juice that has collected on the baking sheet and toss to coat.

To serve, pour ½ cup dressing in a pool on a platter or divide it among four plates. Arrange the tomatoes next to the dressing, top with the parsley mixture, and serve.

Watermelon with Avocado, Chèvre, Basil, and Sweet Onion Vinaigrette

One of my favorite snacks of summer is a slice of ripe watermelon with coarse sea salt. Part of what I love about it is the hunt for the perfect melon: studying the pale side where it rested on the earth, and then thumping it to hear the callback of a bass thud promising ripeness.

All of the other ingredients in this recipe are gilding the lily, if I'm being honest, but sometimes it's fun to have it all. **SERVES 4**

4 (2-inch-thick) slices of ripe watermelon

Sea salt

Black pepper in a mill

2 ripe avocados

4 ounces chèvre

8 fresh basil leaves

¼ cup Sweet Onion Vinaigrette (page 85)

Place a watermelon slice on each of four plates and season with salt and freshly ground pepper. Cut each avocado in half, remove the pit, and carefully remove the peel. Thinly slice the avocado halves, leaving ½ inch at the top so that they stay together. Gently press at the center to form a fan. Season each half with sea salt and coarsely ground pepper. Place 1 avocado portion on top of each watermelon slice. Crumble 1 ounce of the chèvre over each plate. Tear the basil leaves into pieces and distribute over the four plates. Drizzle the vinaigrette over each plate and serve.

Avocado Guilt

In Raleigh, we're truly lucky when it comes to local ingredients. We have a vibrant agricultural community, with access to amazing produce (our farmers' market is open seven days a week). In fact, farming continues to be one of the largest occupations in the state. So as a chef, I find that cooking with local ingredients is not only delicious and conscientious but also relatively easy.

With one major exception.

As in most places in the country, avocados don't grow well in North Carolina. There are no local farmers nurturing these delightful and amazing fruits

(quit smirking, California). But avocados are one of my very favorite ingredients, so I justify eating them and having them on the menu at certain times by making sure that when we use them, we respect the shit out of them. Wherever they appear on the Poole's menu, they do so as the star of the dish, the halves featured intact and fanned out with as much attention and care as sliced steak.

Eating 100 percent locally or organically is not an option for most Americans because of time or money or access or some combination of the three. And dogmatic approaches to sourcing can take the joy out of what should be joyful. So I'll continue to celebrate

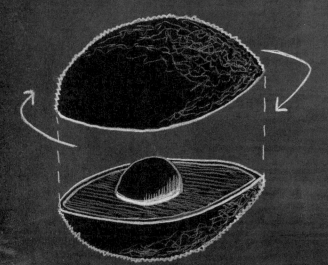

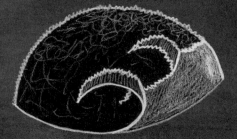

the occasional avocado, letting it stand surrounded by other ingredients grown closer to home, and feeling lucky for the chance to do so.

HERE'S HOW TO FAN AN AVOCADO, POOLE'S-STYLE.

The key is starting with a perfectly ripe avocado, which means you should go shopping a few days prior to making your dish. Let the avocado ripen on the counter until the flesh gives slightly when you press it with one finger. It should not feel mushy to the touch—just slightly tender.

Halve the avocado lengthwise and remove the pit. Place the avocado halves on a cutting board cut side down and carefully remove the peels, trying your best to keep from making indents on the flesh (this will only work if your avocado is truly ripe). Starting ½ inch from the top, make ¼-inch-thick slices down the length of the avocado; take care not to slice through the top so that the whole thing stays together. Press down lightly on the bridge of the fruit so it fans out slightly. Season with salt and pepper.

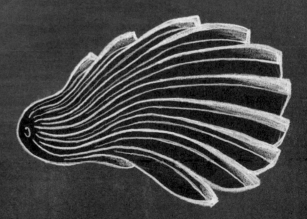

Marinated Avocados with Apples, Blue Cheese, and Almonds

Apples and blue cheese make a natural pair—they prove the "popcorn-chocolate" theory. It's the reason that most of us love salty, buttery popcorn with a rattling box of M&M's at the movie theater: salty-sweet combinations delight the palate. We round out the dish by filling the rest of the chairs in the theater: avocado for creamy richness and subtle fruitiness; almonds for nuttiness and crunch; daikon for water chestnut–like crispness and a touch of rooty vegetal funkiness; and Cider-Sorghum-Dijon Vinaigrette for its piquancy and depth of caramel-amber sweetness. A mandoline is useful here to slice the ingredients uniformly, but a sharp knife will also do the trick. The vinaigrette (which you'll have plenty of) will keep in the fridge for up to 7 days. **SERVES 4, with extra dressing**

CIDER-SORGHUM-DIJON VINAIGRETTE

2 teaspoons minced shallots

⅓ cup cider vinegar

⅓ cup sorghum or maple syrup

⅓ cup whole-grain mustard

2 tablespoons Dijon mustard

1 cup neutral vegetable oil

Sea salt

2 avocados, halved, pitted, and peeled

Sea salt

Black pepper in a mill

Extra-virgin olive oil

1 Pink Lady apple, skin on, cored, and thinly sliced

½ cup thinly sliced daikon radish

2 tablespoons chopped Marcona almonds

½ small red onion, sliced thin

2 ounces creamy blue cheese, crumbled

To make the vinaigrette, place the shallots and vinegar in a small bowl and let soak for at least 15 minutes.

In a large mixing bowl, whisk together the shallots with their vinegar, the syrup, and the mustards until combined. While whisking, slowly add the oil in a thin stream to emulsify. Season with salt to taste.

Thinly slice the avocado halves, leaving ½ inch at the top so that they stay together. Gently press at the center to form a fan. Season with salt and then pepper, then drizzle lightly with olive oil. Place 1 avocado half on each of four plates.

In a small mixing bowl, combine the apple, radish, almonds, onion, cheese, ¼ cup of the vinaigrette, ¼ teaspoon salt, and 10 cranks of the pepper mill. Mix well with a spoon. Divide the salad among the plates, spooning it over the avocado. Garnish with a thin drizzle of olive oil.

Sweet Potatoes with Roasted Poblanos, Chèvre, and Banyuls Vinaigrette

Sweet potatoes are a tremendously prevalent crop where I'm from. So much so that when I traveled to London to cook a Southern-themed dinner, the only sweet potatoes available to cook with were shipped in from North Carolina.

This is a hearty, rib-sticking salad, and it can easily be embraced as a side dish or even a main. The slight spice of the poblanos complements the tubers' sweetness, while tart goat cheese sets the whole thing off. If you've never tried Banyuls vinegar before, it's worth seeking out for its cask-aged depth.

Have leftovers? Pop them into an oven-safe dish and caramelize under your broiler. Serve with sunny-side-up eggs over the top.

SERVES 6 to 8

6 medium sweet potatoes
(about 10 ounces each)

2 whole poblano peppers
(about 4 ounces each)

Sea salt

1 medium red onion

4 ounces chèvre

Black pepper in a mill

¾ cup Banyuls Vinaigrette
(page 85)

Preheat a convection oven to 350°F (or a regular oven to 375°F).

Wash the sweet potatoes and dry with a kitchen towel. Using a fork, poke each potato ten times, evenly distributing your pokes. Place the potatoes on a foil-lined baking sheet and bake until fork tender, 50 to 60 minutes. Let cool for 20 minutes and then, using your hands, carefully peel the skin off of the potatoes, keeping the potatoes whole.

While the potatoes are in the oven, place the peppers directly over a high gas flame. Using metal tongs to safely rotate the peppers, char the entire surface of each pepper. My final step in this process is to balance the pepper on its curvy stem end on the grate of the burner to char that part. This ensures the best yield. (If you don't have a gas range, roast the peppers under an oven broiler set on high, rotating them with metal tongs so they char evenly.)

Transfer the roasted peppers to a metal bowl and cover tightly with plastic wrap. Let sit for 15 minutes. Use a kitchen towel to gently rub off the skins of the peppers; don't run them under water as this will wash away some of the flavor. It's careful work, but it's worth it. Next, tear the peppers in half and remove the stems and seeds. Cut the peppers into ¼-inch squares. Place the peppers in a bowl and season with ¼ teaspoon sea salt, and set aside.

Place a cast-iron skillet over medium-high heat and use a paper towel to rub the interior of the pan with a fine layer of vegetable oil. Slice the red onion across the equator into ½-inch-thick slabs. Season the face of each slab of onion generously with sea salt, and place the seasoned side down in the preheated skillet. Cook until the face of each onion slab is charred, 5 to 6 minutes. Remove the onion slabs from the pan and let them rest with the charred side up. Once they cool to room temperature, slice each slab from top to bottom and then from left to right (imagine a tic-tac-toe grid) into ¼-inch squares. Add to the bowl of roasted poblanos along with ¼ cup of the vinaigrette and thoroughly mix together.

Slice the sweet potatoes into ¾-inch-thick coins and lay flat on a serving dish. Season the face of the potatoes with sea salt and freshly cracked pepper. Scatter the poblano and onion mixture over the sweet potatoes, covering as much of the surface as you can. Crumble the chèvre over the top. Drizzle the remaining ½ cup vinaigrette evenly over the surface of the dish and serve.

Warm Broccoli Salad with Cheddar and Bacon Vinaigrette

This salad adheres pretty faithfully to the vibes of a classic broccoli salad, right down to the halved grapes. But aged crumbly cheddar, toasted pecan halves, and a warm, rich bacon vinaigrette takes it from typical to transcendent. I pull this recipe out every winter, as it caters to my craving for crunchy vegetables while also providing warm, hearty satisfaction (thanks, bacon). **SERVES 6 to 8**

¾ cup kosher salt

8 cups ice

1 bunch broccoli (about 1¼ pounds), ends trimmed

½ cup pecan halves

4 ounces bacon, diced

2 tablespoons olive oil

1 teaspoon Dijon mustard

2 tablespoons red wine vinegar

4 green onions, white parts only, chopped

Black pepper in a mill

1 cup halved red seedless grapes

4 ounces aged white cheddar, sliced thin and crumbled

In a large pot, combine 4 quarts water with ½ cup of the kosher salt; bring to a boil. In a large bowl, combine 2 quarts water with the ice and the remaining ¼ cup kosher salt. Set the bowl within easy reach of the stove.

Cut the broccoli stems from the heads; slice the florets into small pieces, each about 1 inch long. Peel the stems with a peeler and cut each stem in half lengthwise, then slice into ½-inch-thick half-moons. Add the broccoli to the boiling water and blanch for 30 seconds; transfer to the ice water to shock. Drain in a colander and set aside (still in the colander) to drain completely.

In a large dry skillet, toast the pecans over medium heat until they smell aromatic and nutty, about 1 minute. Set aside. Return the skillet to medium heat and add the bacon and oil. Cook until the bacon has rendered its fat and is crispy, about 10 minutes. Turn the heat to low and whisk the mustard and vinegar into the bacon and bacon fat, then add the green onions and pecans and season with 12 cranks of the pepper mill. Toss to coat.

In a large bowl, combine the broccoli and grapes. Pour the contents of the skillet into the bowl and toss to combine. Sprinkle with the cheddar and toss right before serving.

Lamb Carpaccio with Roasted Tomato, Crispy Artichokes, and Yogurt Vinaigrette

There's no lettuce in this recipe, but it might be the most perfect definition of "salad" there is. Each component comes together to make a bite that ranges from gamey to crunchy, salty to sweet, tangy to creamy. We served it during the dinner we cooked at the James Beard House, and it was later recognized by the foundation as one of the best dishes served there all year.

Don't be intimidated by the idea of raw meat. The only hard-and-fast rule is that you need to use the best possible lamb you can get your hands on for this dish, purchased from a trusted source. Freezing the lamb before serving it rids the meat of any unwanted bacteria, much as cooking it would.

Continued

You can prepare all the components in advance of assembly; once prepped, the dish comes together in minutes. **SERVES 4**

1½ pounds boneless lamb loin,
very cold

Neutral vegetable oil, for frying

1 cup frozen artichoke hearts

¼ cup full-fat plain Greek yogurt

2 tablespoons buttermilk

Sea salt

Black pepper in a mill

Olive oil

Fresh lemon juice

1 cup Roasted Tomato Relish
(page 162)

1 cup oil-cured olives, drained
and minced

Trim the lamb of any gristle, tendons, or silver skin and slice into ¼-inch-thick slices; transfer to the freezer for 10 minutes to chill.

Cut along the sides of four 1-gallon resealable plastic bags, leaving the bottoms intact (each will look like one long sheet of plastic). Spread one of the plastic bags flat on a work surface and arrange a quarter of the lamb in the center of one-half (so you can fold the other half over the top of the lamb to cover). The lamb should be in a flat layer with the edges of each slice just barely overlapping its neighbor. Fold the plastic over to cover the lamb and, using a meat pounder, pound out the lamb into a very thin single layer. Individual slices might want to spread out away from the other pieces as you pound; push them back into a cohesive layer with the other pieces. Place the carpaccio (still between the plastic bag layers) on a baking sheet and store in the freezer. Repeat with the remaining lamb so that you have four layers of carpaccio. Freeze until 10 minutes before you're ready to use.

To make the crispy artichokes, line a plate with paper towels. Pour 2 inches of neutral vegetable oil into a heavy-bottomed pot and set over high heat until the oil reaches 350°F on a deep-fry thermometer. Thinly slice the (still-frozen) artichoke hearts and add to the oil. Fry for 2 minutes, or until crispy; as they finish, transfer the artichoke crisps to the lined plate and season lightly with salt.

Ten minutes before you're ready to serve, remove the lamb from the freezer. Transfer one serving to a work surface and peel back the plastic from the top. Place the carpaccio, exposed side down, onto a plate, then peel off the plastic. Repeat with the remaining servings and let sit for 5 minutes to thaw.

Meanwhile, in a small bowl, whisk together the yogurt and buttermilk and season with ⅛ teaspoon salt.

Season the surface of each carpaccio generously with salt and pepper and drizzle with olive oil and a squeeze of lemon juice. Scatter some of the artichokes over the surface of each plate, then sprinkle with some of the tomato relish and olives. Finish the dish by drizzling 1 to 2 tablespoons of the yogurt vinaigrette over the carpaccio.

Beet Salad with Fromage Blanc and Burnt Orange Marmalade Vinaigrette

MISTER-POTATO-HEAD YOUR ROASTED BEET SALAD

Using roasted beets as a base, here are some of my favorite beet salad combinations:

- Roasted beets with burrata, burnt orange marmalade vinaigrette, and pistachios

- Roasted beets with crispy prosciutto, chèvre, and cider-sorghum-Dijon vinaigrette

- Roasted beets with chickpeas, mint, mizuna, burnt orange marmalade vinaigrette, and crème fraîche

- Roasted beets with crispy bacon, arugula, blue cheese, and banyuls vinaigrette

Beets have plenty of haters. There are those who hate them because they grew up eating the canned version, and they can't divorce that bland, mushy childhood memory from the actual ingredient. Then there's the beet and goat cheese salad, which became a cliché of 1990s restaurant cooking and now inspires sneering among those who take food too seriously. I've also heard complaints that beets taste "like dirt" and that they are just too earthy for some taste buds.

Personally, I love beets, so much so that they are almost always featured as part of a salad on the Poole's menu. Seriously—once one of the cooks in the kitchen remarked that the current menu didn't have a beet salad, and we all stared at one another in horror. (We immediately resolved the issue by coming up with a beet, burrata, and pistachio salad that stole the show.)

I've made endless variations of beet salads over the years, and have proudly convinced a good number of former beet haters to come over into the beet-loving light. So much about beets' bad reputations can be remedied with care in the kitchen: roast them to tenderness but not mush, make sure to pair them with ingredients that complement (rather than exaggerate) their earthiness, and allow yourself to break out of the goat cheese mold (though it's delicious, everyone needs some variety). Problems solved.

I chose to include this particular salad because it's both simple and delicious—a perfect beet salad introduction for the nonbelievers. There's something very natural about oranges and beets, and caramelizing the orange marmalade before adding it to the vinaigrette provides a little bitterness that helps balance the sweetness of the dish. Fromage blanc is a creamy, neutral fresh cheese that provides richness without overpowering the other ingredients. As with other salads in this chapter, you'll make more vinaigrette than you'll need for this salad, and you will not be sorry you did. The Burnt Orange Marmalade Vinaigrette will keep in the fridge for 2 weeks. **SERVES 6 to 8, with extra dressing**

BURNT ORANGE MARMALADE VINAIGRETTE

2 oranges, sliced in half from pole to pole

½ cup sugar

Sea salt

2 tablespoons champagne vinegar

1⅓ cups Red Wine Vinaigrette (page 84)

2 pounds medium beets, tops removed

½ red onion, thinly sliced

Sea salt

Black pepper in a mill

4 ounces fromage blanc

To make the vinaigrette, use a paper towel and tongs to rub the interior of a cast-iron skillet with a thin layer of neutral vegetable oil and place over high heat. When the pan is very hot, place the orange halves cut side down in the pan and cook, undisturbed, until they have charred and caramelized, about 6 minutes. Transfer to a cutting board and let cool. When the oranges are cool enough to handle, use a spoon to scoop the flesh from the rind. Thinly slice the rind into slivers and set aside. Place the flesh in a food processor and puree; strain through a fine-mesh sieve over a bowl, discarding the solids.

In a medium saucepot, bring the orange rind, sugar, a pinch of salt, champagne vinegar, and strained juice to a simmer, stirring to dissolve the sugar. Cook until thick, 15 to 20 minutes or until the marmalade reaches 218°F on a thermometer. Let cool completely.

Measure 2 tablespoons of the Red Wine Vinaigrette and set aside. Place the remaining vinaigrette in a mixing bowl and whisk in ¾ cup of the marmalade until the mixture is completely combined. Season to taste with salt. Store in a lidded container in the refrigerator until ready to use. Leftover marmalade will keep in the refrigerator for up to 1 month.

To roast the beets, preheat a convection oven to 375°F (or a regular oven to 400°F). Pour ¼ inch of water into a 13-by-9-inch baking dish. Add the beets and cover the pan securely with foil. Transfer to the oven and cook for 60 to 90 minutes, until a knife can be easily inserted into the beets. Let sit until cool enough to handle, then rub the skins from the beets with a paper towel. (The beets can be roasted up to 2 days ahead and stored in sealed plastic bags in the refrigerator. Let come to room temperature before using.)

Slice the beets into ¼-inch-thick slices and place in a large bowl. Add the onion and season to taste with salt and a few cranks of the pepper mill. Add the reserved 2 tablespoons Red Wine Vinaigrette and toss gently to coat. Place the contents of the bowl on a platter and use a spoon to dollop the fromage blanc over the top. Drizzle about ¾ cup of the marmalade vinaigrette over the top of the salad and serve.

Vegetables

As excited as I am to share all of the recipes in this book, this is the chapter I could live in. Vegetables are where I'm most comfortable, most at ease, as a cook and an eater. And I believe that when we deck the table with a spread of thoughtful vegetable-based dishes, meat is seldom missed. On road trips across the South when I was a child, we stopped at meat-and-threes for plates of vegetables, always preferring the sides on offer over the meat mains.

As a cook, my internal calendar has always run by the colors and varieties of vegetables in my kitchen. Pumpkin-orange butternut squash and deep green braised collards tell me that the trees are bare and the air is cold. Bright red tomatoes and sunshine yellow summer squashes assure me that the days have gotten longer and that short sleeves are the way to go. There is no finer harbinger of any season than its crops of vegetables.

There's also no finer medium for stories and conversation. In the agrarian South, in particular, our history is written in the crops we cook and eat. And as the country as a whole continues to return to an alignment between our plates and the seasons, farmers' markets and greenmarkets have become our new food storytellers.

In 2012, I was invited to cook the Saturday lunch at the Southern Foodways Alliance's annual symposium. The lunch is arguably the keynote meal of a very full weekend, and it spotlights just one chef. It's a technical challenge—there's no kitchen from which to serve the meal—as well as a mental one. Each year, the four hundred people in attendance are some of the most enthusiastic, seasoned, intelligent, and respected minds (and mouths) in our community. So I was cooking for an audience of peers and critics, colleagues and academics who had come to expect great things from this lunch in years past.

The theme was barbecue—a topic as loaded as politics and religion. As I began to think about what I would do, it occurred to me that my favorite part of any barbecue spread has always been the dishes that surround the plate of smoked meat: the slaws, the cornbread, the potato salad. I had a wild idea to present a lunch that was inspired by these dishes—and was free of meat. That's right. A vegetarian lunch at a barbecue weekend. (I woke up more than once in the middle of the night asking myself if I was nuts.)

We prepped for weeks, loaded up a van with coolers, and drove to Mississippi. On the day of the lunch, as we sent out the last round of plates, I peeked into the cavernous hall to see how my ambitious plan was playing out. As the family-style dishes hit the tables, the guests dug in spoons and passed pie tins. With each course, conversations erupted: "I've had these peas, but we don't call them White Acres in Alabama." "You can BBQ popcorn?" "What the heck is corn cream? And can I have more of it?" "Pass the pimento." "Are you gonna finish those mustard greens?" In ninety minutes, twelve courses had been passed, shared, enjoyed, and discussed. There was no rumble over the absence of meat, only jubilation over the awesomeness of a story told by a cast of vegetables, each called by one name or another, depending on where you call home.

The menu we served that day is on the next page.

Marinated White Acre Peas

Field peas keep beautifully when frozen. I have a farmer friend who, after his meemaw (grandmother) passed away, discovered a baggie of heirloom field peas in her chest freezer. There was a tiny note in the bag with the peas: "polecat pea, 1984." My friend decided to plant the peas to see if they'd grow; at harvest he was rewarded with buckets of a new crop of his grandmother's decades-old peas.

Of all the field peas, White Acres are my favorite, and every summer we buy and freeze as many as we can to use throughout the year when fresh peas aren't available. It's a running joke in the kitchen that we're always on "the last bag" of field peas, something that I think we say to remind everyone of how limited our supply is, and how special the ingredient.

In that vein, this is one of my favorite ways to serve field peas because it lets them shine. The key to a perfectly seasoned pea is to stir in the salt after the cooking and let them come down to room temperature in their cooking liquid. **SERVES 6 to 8**

4 cups fresh or frozen White Acre peas (or other petite lady peas)

2 tablespoons kosher salt

A large sachet (see page 18)

½ cup minced celery

½ cup minced red onion

½ cup coarsely chopped fresh parsley

1 cup Banyuls Vinaigrette (see page 85)

Black pepper in a mill

Rinse the peas, place in a pot, and cover with 6 cups cool water. Bring to boil over high heat, then reduce to a simmer and cook until tender, 25 to 30 minutes. The peas should still hold their shape but be tender throughout. Stir in the salt, add the sachet, and remove from the heat. Allow the peas to cool to room temperature in the cooking liquid. Once cool, drain the peas, discard the sachet, and transfer the peas to a mixing bowl.

Add the celery, onion, and parsley to the bowl of peas. Pour the vinaigrette over the peas and stir to coat. Let the peas marinate at room temperature for 1 hour, stirring to coat every 15 minutes. Season with black pepper to taste.

Serve at room temperature.

Luck and Money

On New Year's Day, every year, my mother's sole focus is making sure that we get our peas and greens. It's not a suggestion; it's a must. I've always loved this, as my mother has never been one for superstitions. (She is very clear to tell me, "This isn't superstition—this is tradition.") This offering is said to symbolize luck and money, but to me it's more.

I think of January as a time to let the year know that you're coming for it, in a take no prisoners kind of way. So for me, this dish isn't about accumulating luck or money: *it's about not letting either stand in your way*. And through that we find health and prosperity, opportunity and happiness, satisfaction and greatness. All of that in a little bowl of peas and greens? Tradition or superstition, it's a lot to be grateful for.

We serve this dish at Poole's throughout the month of January. We braise winter greens with onions, garlic, and chile and deglaze the pan with cider vinegar. We stir in some Sea Island red peas, which have a bit more earthiness than traditional black-eyed peas, and we top the dish with a roasted garlic compound butter and pepper. **SERVES 6 to 8**

2 cups dried Sea Island red peas, rinsed

A small sachet (page 18)

Kosher salt

¼ cup neutral vegetable oil

1 yellow onion, minced

2 pounds collard greens, stemmed and chopped (reserve stems for pickling)

Sea salt

1 teaspoon dried chile flakes, toasted

½ cup dry white wine

¼ cup cider vinegar

2 tablespoons Roasted Garlic Butter (page 20)

Black pepper in a mill

Place the peas in a large bowl, cover with cold water, and let soak for 3 hours. Drain the peas and transfer to a large stockpot. Add 2 quarts cold water and the sachet and bring to a boil over high heat. Reduce to a simmer and cook until the peas are tender but still holding their shape, about 30 minutes. Remove from the heat and stir in 1 tablespoon salt. Let the peas cool in their cooking liquid to room temperature.

In a large stockpot over medium heat, warm the oil. Add the onion and cook until softened, 5 to 7 minutes. Add the greens and stir to coat with the onions and oil. Season lightly with sea salt and chile flakes. Stir for 2 minutes to let the seasoning permeate the ingredients. Add the wine and cook, stirring every few minutes, until the greens are very tender and breaking down slightly, 30 to 40 minutes. Meanwhile, drain the peas, reserving 1 cup of the cooking liquid.

Once the greens are tender, stir in the cooked peas and vinegar. Bring to a simmer and add the garlic butter. Season with salt to taste and a few cranks of the pepper mill. If the mixture is looking dry, add the reserved pea liquid by the tablespoon. Simmer for 10 more minutes, allowing all of the ingredients to come together.

There is nothing revolutionary about this dish. It's really quite humble; that, to me, is what makes it so good. I came up with this recipe on a rainy weekend in early fall. It was the first cool snap of the season, the kind of day that gets you excited about all of the braises and stews you forgot about over the summer. A simple pot of lentils, mixed in with slowly melted leeks and seasoned with a healthy dose of lemon was the perfect way to welcome the weather. Serve it as the hearty, comforting base to the Pan-Roasted Scallops with Olive Gremolata on page 226; top it with a poached egg and a sprinkle of chile flakes for a satisfying autumn brunch; or gild the lily by stirring in a spoonful of homemade crème fraîche (page 159). **SERVES 6 to 8**

1 cup beluga or French
    green lentils, rinsed

A small sachet (see page 18)

Sea salt

6 medium leeks

2 tablespoons neutral vegetable oil

1 tablespoon unsalted butter

Juice and zest of 1 lemon

1 tablespoon olive oil

Black pepper in a mill

Place the lentils in a medium saucepan with 5 cups water and the sachet. Bring to a boil, then reduce to a simmer. Cook at a simmer until the lentils are tender but not mushy and holding their shape, about 20 minutes. Remove from the heat and stir in 1 teaspoon salt. Let the lentils cool in their cooking liquid to room temperature.

Meanwhile, prepare the leeks. Trim the root ends of each leek and cut the dark green tops off ¼ inch below where the leaves begin to split at the stalk. Compost the greens (or save them for making stock). Slice each leek in half lengthwise, then thinly slice crosswise to form half-moons (you should have about 4 cups sliced leeks). Break the leek rings up with your fingers and place in a colander. Clean well under cold water; leeks hold a lot of dirt that will make your dish taste gritty if you're not thorough.

In a Dutch oven over medium heat, heat the oil. When it shimmers, add the leeks and 1 teaspoon salt. Stir, cooking, for about 1 minute, then cover and cook for 15 minutes, stirring once at about 10 minutes. Remove the pan from the heat and let sit, covered, for 10 minutes more.

When the lentils have reached room temperature, drain them, reserving the liquid. Add the lentils and ¾ cup of the reserved liquid to the pan with the leeks and place over high heat. Bring to a simmer, then stir in the butter. When the butter has melted and is thoroughly incorporated, turn off the heat and stir in the lemon juice and zest and the olive oil. Season generously with pepper (20 cranks of the mill) and serve.

Oyster Mushrooms and Asparagus with Sherry and Cream

Oyster mushrooms are in the sweet spot of the fungi world; they're meaty like shiitakes, mild like portobellos, buttery like chanterelles, and affordable like creminis, all in one single varietal. Mushrooms hold a good amount of moisture, so it's important to season them with salt *after* you've seared them to let some of that liquid evaporate. This will ensure that your mushrooms caramelize a little bit before getting tossed with sherry and cream. **SERVES 8**

3 tablespoons neutral vegetable oil

2 pounds oyster mushrooms, tough stems removed, torn into bite-size pieces

Sea salt

¼ cup minced shallots

4 thyme sprigs

2 pounds asparagus, ends trimmed and cut into 2-inch pieces

1 cup amontillado sherry (I like Lustau)

¾ cup heavy cream

2 tablespoons cold unsalted butter, cut into cubes

2 tablespoons Porcini Butter (page 20)

Juice of ½ lemon

In a large skillet, heat the oil over medium heat. Add the mushrooms and let sear, stirring a few times, until the moisture they release has evaporated and the edges begin to crisp and they get caramelized. Season lightly with salt.

Add the shallots and thyme and cook for 1 minute, stirring to combine and coat everything. Stir in the asparagus, then add the sherry and deglaze the pan by swirling and scraping the bottom of the pan to release any browned bits. Cook until the liquid is reduced by three-quarters, stirring occasionally; this will take about 3 minutes. Add the cream and let it reduce until it's thickened slightly and coats the asparagus and mushrooms, about another 2 minutes. Remove from the heat and stir in the cold butters.

Stir in the lemon juice, season with salt to taste, and serve immediately.

The Chalkboard Menu

At Poole's, the menus aren't printed. They aren't available on our website. Instead they are handwritten on giant mural-size chalkboards that line the walls of the space. This started out as a way to highlight the seasonality of our approach and keep the menu spontaneous. It felt like it both fit with the space and harkened back to the era of daily specials on the board, a recognizable feature of diners, luncheonettes, and meat-and-threes across the South.

But we couldn't have foreseen the effect they would have on the experience of dining at Poole's. Much like the double-horseshoe bar, the chalkboards are focal points of the room. People get out of their seats to take a closer look, and in doing so, find themselves in close proximity to another table. Conversations start up; people get to know one another. It's not a forced interaction or intimacy, just a small moment that happens over and over every night, adding to the energy of the space.

Very few of the dishes have permanent status on the chalkboard (Macaroni au Gratin on page 190 and Pimento Cheese on page 33 are two). We have several anchor dishes that might be available most of the year, however, with ingredients swapped out to honor the seasons. Tomato pie, for example, will become an onion-Gruyère tart come winter; or the beet salad might have burrata and peaches in the summer, blue cheese and country ham in the winter. The preparation is similar, but the featured ingredients change.

But there's perhaps no better example of our approach to seasonality than oyster mushrooms with sherry and cream (see page 129). Using that basic template, you can highlight a huge array of vegetables, and somehow that cloak of sherry and cream works with all of them. The version in this book uses asparagus, but we've made the dish with cauliflower, sugar snap peas, corn, and brussels sprouts. Each time, it's like a new dish, revived and revitalized; different nuances emerge in the flavors depending on the ingredient at the center.

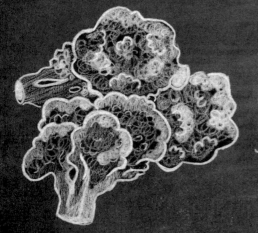

CAULIFLOWER

In a large saucepan, combine 2 quarts milk and
2 quarts water. Add 6 tablespoons kosher salt and
bring to a simmer. Add the florets from 2 heads
of cauliflower and cook until barely tender, about
2 minutes. Drain very well and transfer to a baking
sheet to cool. Proceed with the recipe on page 129,
using the cauliflower in place of the asparagus.

CORN

Shuck 10 ears of fresh corn and cut off the kernels;
save the cobs for another use (such as making Chilled
Corn Soup with Cherry Tomatoes on page 170).
Proceed with the recipe on page 129, using the corn
in place of the asparagus.

BRUSSELS SPROUTS

Peel the outer tough layers from 2 pounds brussels
sprouts. Remove and discard the base of the sprout
and separate the leaves. Proceed with the recipe on
page 129, using the brussels sprouts in place of the
asparagus.

SUGAR SNAP PEAS

Trim the ends of 2 pounds sugar snap peas and
remove the tough belly strings. Halve on the
diagonal. Proceed with the recipe on page 129,
using the snap peas in place of the asparagus.

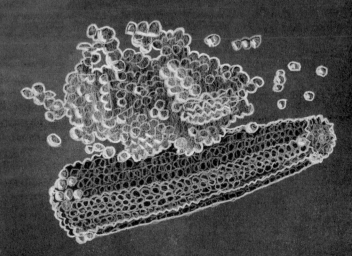

Cornmeal-Fried Okra with Tabasco Mayo

Both okra and deep-frying are key pillars of Southern cooking, but they share another trait: they can be intimidating to home cooks. If the idea of okra or deep-frying (or both) makes you uneasy, this recipe is your reassurance. It's both simple enough and delicious enough to help you move past your fears. Plus, the technique is extremely versatile, and it works seamlessly with a plethora of vegetables and seafood.

The most important step in frying is confidence. A lot of folks are afraid of hot oil, so they tend to keep plenty of space from it, pitching ingredients into the pot like they're shooting free throws. Doing so causes the hot oil to splash, which highly increases your chance of getting burned. Please don't do this! Instead, be the boss: get close enough to the pot to gently release the battered item into the fryer, whether you're using a fry basket or your hands. This allows the oil temperature to adjust to the lower temperature of your ingredients, which keeps it from spattering and splashing. One more note about frying: a deep-fry thermometer is your best friend. If the oil isn't hot enough, it will saturate whatever you're frying, turning it into a greasy mess. If your oil is too hot, it will cook the exterior faster than the interior, giving your food a burnt flavor. And of course, the temperature of your oil will fluctuate, making this whole process a little bit of a balancing act—it will lower when you add your ingredients; it will creep up if you leave the heat on high the whole time. The only way to know where you stand and guarantee success is by following your thermometer. Do not attempt this or any frying recipe without one.

In the old school approach to fried okra, the okra pods are cut into coins before being battered and fried. This style is delicious and crispy, but you tend to taste more of the batter than the okra, which, to me, sort of undermines the beauty of the dish. I cut the okra in half lengthwise, a shape that mimics French fries and makes it highly suitable for dipping in a condiment of your choosing.

I suggest serving the okra with Tabasco mayo, which presents a flavorful heat without firebombing your palate. Mayo of any persuasion complements this crispy dish, but serve it with any condiment that floats your boat. Remember, you're the boss.

Green tomatoes play well by this same approach. I like to slice them in wedges (as opposed to the traditional sandwich-style slices), so that the center of the wedge stays tart and fruity and the outsides get rich and burnished. **SERVES 6 to 8**

Continued

TABASCO MAYO

1 cup Tabasco

2 cups Basic Cider Mayo
(page 21)

2 cups buttermilk

2 cups cornmeal

2 teaspoons sea salt

Neutral vegetable oil, for frying

1 pound okra, trimmed and
sliced lengthwise

To make the mayo, in a small saucepan over medium heat, bring the Tabasco to a simmer and reduce by half. Let cool completely. Stir the Tabasco reduction into the mayo and store in a lidded container in the refrigerator until ready to use.

Place the buttermilk in a shallow mixing bowl. Place the cornmeal and salt in a second large mixing bowl.

Line a baking sheet with two or three layers of paper towel. Pour oil into a large, heavy-bottomed pot or Dutch oven, filling it about half full. Heat the oil over high heat until it reaches 325°F on a deep-fry thermometer.

When the oil is hot, dredge and fry the okra. Working in batches, put the okra in the buttermilk and use a spoon or your hands to coat it completely. Remove the okra, letting any excess buttermilk drip back into the bowl, then transfer to the cornmeal and toss to completely coat. Pull the okra from the cornmeal and gently place it in the hot oil. Fry each batch for 3 to 4 minutes, turning occasionally with tongs, until the crust on each piece is golden brown. As the okra finishes, transfer it to the prepared baking sheet to drain briefly, then serve immediately with the Tabasco mayo. Repeat with the remaining okra in batches, keeping it coming fresh and hot to your guests.

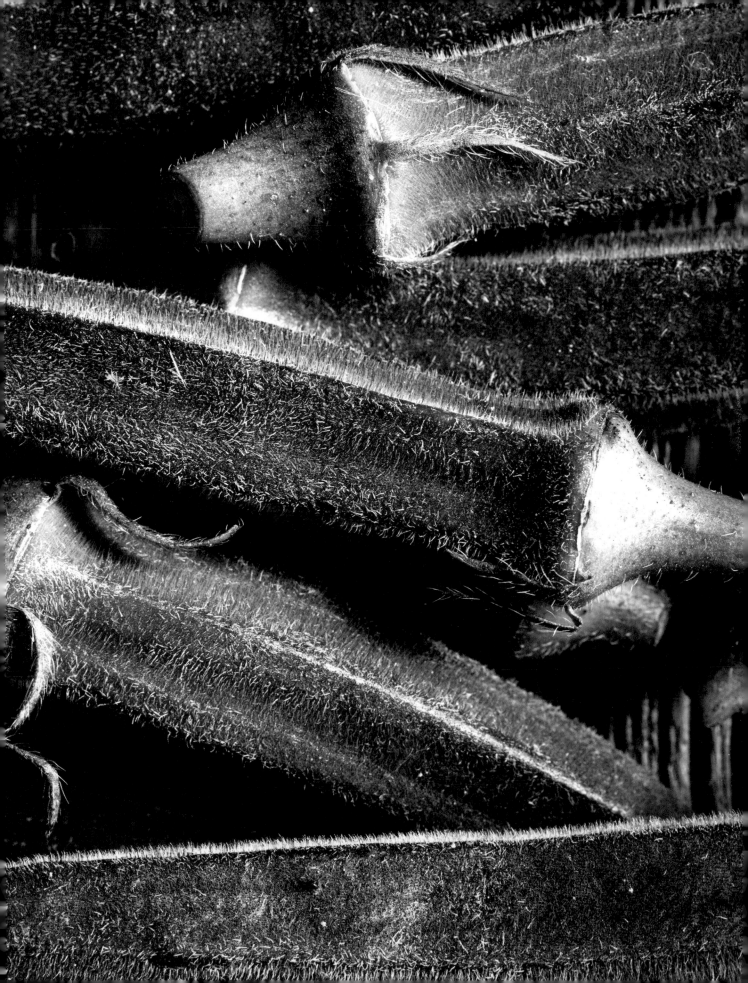

Wilted Greens with Olive Oil and Garlic

When most people think of comfort food, they think of the heavy stuff: the mashed potatoes and fried chicken, the meatloaf and mac and cheese. Clearly, I love those dishes as much as anyone (pages 151, 205, 232, and 190). But this quick and simple recipe for sautéed greens with garlic might make me most "comfortable" of all. I simply *feel* good when I eat a plate of hearty greens; it's like a dose of energy to my system. Additionally, I crave their bright, slightly bitter vegetal flavor to combat the intensity of proteins like pork and beef.

The key to this recipe is to season liberally; greens can need a fair amount of salt to reach that perfect point of flavor. Once you add your greens to the pan, keep them moving; they will cook rather quickly. You can use a single type of green or a mixture: some of my favorites include kale, Swiss chard, spinach, collards, and tatsoi. **SERVES 4**

2 tablespoons neutral vegetable oil

4 cloves garlic, thinly sliced

¼ teaspoon chile flakes

1 pound braising greens such as collards or chard or a mixture, torn

Sea salt

1 tablespoon cold unsalted butter

1½ teaspoons olive oil

Juice of ½ lemon

In a skillet or wok over medium heat, warm the vegetable oil. When it shimmers, add the garlic and toast, swirling the pan constantly, until golden brown and fragrant, about 1 minute. It should not darken in color. Add the chile flakes and cook, stirring, for 15 seconds. Add the greens and season with salt. Keep the pan and your spoon moving constantly and cook for 2 to 3 minutes; heartier greens (such as kale or collards) will need the extra minute. Taste the greens to check for desired tenderness and seasoning. Remove from the heat and stir in the butter, olive oil, and lemon juice. Serve immediately.

Charred Summer Squash with Fresh Herbs

In so many households, home cooks have subjected carrots or broccoli to long cooking times, rendering them meltingly soft (or "mushy" to those less partial than I). I always loved the stewed vegetables we had on our table, particularly summer squash, which has an undeniable earthy sweetness when exposed to heat.

This recipe aims to re-create some of my favorite things about that childhood dish, albeit achieved through different means. It embraces the innate sweetness of the squash through a high-heat char rather than a low-heat stew. Charring also creates a handful of textures.

I serve this dish at room temperature because I think it elevates the bright flavors; it also eliminates the rush to eat something while it's hot. Eating and sharing food should be fun, peaceful, and conducive to conversation whenever possible. This dish won't be compromised if left to rest through heated conversations or long-winded celebratory toasts. It's particularly exceptional under fried fish or soft shell crabs. The herbs called for are only suggestions; they can all be subbed out for herbs of your preference. **SERVES 6 to 8**

4 pounds assorted summer squashes, trimmed

2 medium Vidalia onions, halved across the equator

Sea salt

Black pepper in a mill

Juice of 1 lemon

Extra-virgin olive oil

12 fresh basil leaves, torn

8 fresh mint leaves, torn

½ cup fresh parsley leaves, torn

Preheat a cast-iron skillet over medium-high heat.

Slice each squash in half lengthwise (or pole to pole). Season the cut sides of all of the vegetables with sea salt and a few cranks of the pepper mill. Use a paper towel and a pair of tongs to coat the interior of the hot cast-iron pan with a thin layer of neutral vegetable oil. Starting with the onions and working in batches, place the vegetables, cut side down, in the pan. Let cook until the cut surfaces of the vegetables are darkly charred, about 5 minutes. The vegetables should still be crisp (al dente) at the core. Turn them to the other side for 1 minute to soften a bit more and then transfer the vegetables to a baking sheet. Repeat with any remaining vegetables, adding additional oil between batches.

Let the vegetables cool to room temperature. Slice them into bite-size pieces, being sure to remove the root ends. Transfer to a mixing bowl and season with salt, pepper, lemon juice, and olive oil to coat. Fold in the fresh herbs and serve at room temperature.

Rutabaga with Brown Butter and Thyme

The rutabaga is a magical vegetable. A delicious cross of spicy turnips with a hint of rich and silky sweet potato, it's a superhero root with endless applications. I love it sliced paper-thin or julienned in raw vegetable salads and slaws. And it's game-changing when roasted.

In this recipe, roasted rutabagas are crisped in nutty brown butter. Sprigs of thyme scent the brown butter, but because it's not picked or chopped, it doesn't steal the show or overpower the dish. Rutabaga has always been one of those dishes we have to talk guests into ordering, and it quickly cultivates lifelong fans. I love an underdog, and rutabaga leads the pack for sneak attack success. **SERVES 6 to 8**

2½ pounds medium rutabagas (about 4), peeled, quartered and sliced ½ inch thick

1 tablespoon olive oil

Sea salt

11 thyme sprigs

2 tablespoons neutral vegetable oil

2 tablespoons unsalted butter

1 teaspoon fresh lemon juice

Preheat a convection oven to 350°F (or a regular oven to 375°F). Line a baking sheet with parchment paper.

In a large bowl, drizzle the rutabaga with olive oil and sprinkle with 1 teaspoon salt. Add 5 of the thyme sprigs and toss to coat. Arrange the rutabaga slices on the prepared baking sheet and cover tightly with foil. Bake for 30 minutes, rotating the pan 180 degrees every 10 minutes, until the rutabaga is fork-tender. Remove from the oven.

In a large skillet over high heat, add 1 tablespoon of the neutral vegetable oil. Season both sides of the rutabaga slices lightly with salt. When the oil is hot, add half the rutabaga slices to the pan in a single layer, broadest side down, along with 3 of the thyme sprigs. Cook for about 90 seconds, then add 1 tablespoon of the butter, swirling and agitating the pan to help it disperse. Cook, moving the pan, for about 1 minute; the butter will begin to smell toasty and will darken slightly in color. Flip the rutabaga pieces and cook for 1 minute more. Transfer the rutabaga to a platter and drizzle with 1 tablespoon of the butter from the pan; cover with foil to keep warm.

Wipe out the skillet and repeat with the remaining oil, rutabaga, thyme, and butter. To serve, drizzle with the lemon juice.

Pit Peas

Baked beans are a classic side at barbecues everywhere (note: at this very moment, a Southern pit master is cursing me for referring to *barbecue* as an event rather than a food). Even when scooped out of a can, they are as dependable a staple as hamburgers and hot dogs when it comes to a Sunday grill-out.

This recipe is inspired by those nostalgia-inducing spoonfuls of bacony, brown sugary–sweet, grill-side beans. We've replaced the typical brown sugar with sorghum for a warmer depth, and tiny Sea Island red peas stand in for the classic navy bean. These little peas bleed a clay-red liquor that's full of earthiness. (If you can't score Sea Island red peas, which are available online through Anson Mills, sub in dried crowder peas.) **SERVES 8 to 10**

2 cups dried Sea Island red peas, rinsed

A large sachet (see page 18)

Kosher salt

6 tablespoons rendered bacon fat

2 cups minced yellow onion

1 cup minced celery

5 cloves garlic, smashed and crushed into a paste with kosher salt

Sea salt

1 tablespoon freshly ground black pepper

½ cup tomato paste

⅓ cup red wine vinegar

⅔ cup sorghum

½ cup plus 1 tablespoon Dijon mustard

1 teaspoon hot sauce (preferably Texas Pete)

1 teaspoon Worcestershire

2 tablespoons cold Roasted Garlic Butter (page 20), cut into cubes

Place the peas in a large bowl, cover with cold water, and let soak for 3 hours. Drain the peas and transfer to a large stockpot. Cover with 2 quarts cold water and the sachet and bring to a boil over high heat. Reduce to a simmer and cook until the peas are tender but still holding their shape, about 30 minutes. Remove from the heat and stir in 1 tablespoon kosher salt. Let the peas cool in their cooking liquid to room temperature. Drain the peas, reserving 2 cups of the cooking liquid.

Preheat a convection oven to 350°F (or a regular oven to 375°F). In a large Dutch oven over medium heat, combine the bacon fat and onion and cook, stirring often, until they caramelize and turn light golden brown, about 25 minutes. Add the celery and garlic and cook, stirring, until the vegetables have softened, about 6 minutes. Season with 1 teaspoon sea salt and the pepper. Stir in the tomato paste and cook, stirring, for 4 to 5 minutes, until the mixture looks dry and the paste begins to caramelize.

Add the vinegar, scraping up any caramelized bits on the bottom of the pan. Let the vinegar simmer for 1 to 2 minutes to reduce. Stir in the sorghum and bring to a simmer. Stir in the peas and the reserved pea liquid. Bring to a simmer, then stir in the mustard, hot sauce, and Worcestershire. Let simmer on low heat for 20 minutes.

Cover and transfer to the oven. Cook for 30 minutes, then uncover, stir in the garlic butter, and cook for an additional 10 minutes. Let rest for 10 minutes before serving.

Stewed Tomatoes

This is about the simplest thing (save for maybe a tomato sandwich) that you can do with tomatoes, and it's one of the most utilized recipes in the Poole's kitchen. We use it as a base for meat or fish dishes—serve it under Cornbread Crab Cakes (page 225) or alongside Poole's Steak (page 217)—and it's the glue that holds the pork and dumplings (page 186) together.

Like oyster mushrooms with sherry and cream (see page 129), it's also a great base for whatever other vegetables you have on hand. And in the recipe that follows this, I've added charred okra; you can also try it with field peas or sautéed eggplant folded in. **SERVES 12 as a side**

5 pounds Roma tomatoes
(about 20 medium)

Sea salt

1½ pounds yellow onions
(about 2 large), minced

2 tablespoons neutral vegetable oil

A large sachet (see page 18)

Fill a large pot three-quarters full with water and bring to a boil. While the water is coming up, core the tomatoes and, using a sharp knife, make a shallow X-shaped incision on the bottom of each, doing your best to cut just the skin and not into the flesh.

Once the water reaches a boil, prepare an ice bath by filling a large bowl with ice and water; set it within easy reach of the stove. Working in batches, place the tomatoes into the boiling water and cook until the cut skin at the bottom of the tomato begins to stretch and peel away; this usually takes between 45 and 90 seconds. As this happens, transfer the tomatoes one by one to the ice bath. Once the tomatoes are cool, peel their skins off using your hands and set them into a colander in the sink to drain off any excess liquid. Dice the tomatoes into ¾-inch cubes, then place them in a large bowl with 2 teaspoons salt; stir with your hands to combine. Let sit for 20 minutes; the tomatoes will bleed their juices.

In a large, heavy-bottomed pot over medium heat, heat the oil until it shimmers. Add the onions and cook until they have softened, about 5 minutes. Stir in the tomatoes and their liquid and add the sachet. Bring to a simmer and cook until the liquid has mostly evaporated. Taste and adjust the seasoning to your liking. Remove and discard the sachet and serve. The stewed tomatoes will keep for up to 1 week in the refrigerator or 3 months in the freezer.

STEWED TOMATOES AND CHARRED OKRA

1 pound okra, trimmed and sliced in ½-inch-thick coins

Sea salt

4 cups Stewed Tomatoes (see left)

2 tablespoons cold Roasted Garlic Butter (page 20) or regular butter, cut into cubes

Black pepper in a mill

SERVES 6 to 8

Line a plate with a paper towel. Use a paper towel and tongs to wipe the surface of a cast-iron skillet with a thin layer of neutral vegetable oil. Place over high heat for 5 minutes. When the skillet is very hot, add the okra. Let it sear undisturbed for 2 minutes, then stir for 1 minute more to char evenly. Transfer to the paper towel–lined plate and season with salt.

Place the stewed tomatoes in a saucepan over medium heat. When the tomatoes begin to just barely simmer, fold in the okra. Add the butter and remove the pan from the heat. Stir until the butter has completely melted. Season to taste with additional salt and with pepper if needed and serve.

Sautéed Broccoli with Red Wine and Garlic

This recipe is as simple as simple gets, but I think we can all agree that a lot of the best things in life are. It came about as a serendipitous discovery I made one night at home while sautéing broccoli to serve next to a steak. I was priming for the evening with a delicious glass of Beaujolais. I toasted my garlic and then tossed the broccoli into the garlic-scented oil. A few moments later, I reached for a bottle of white wine to deglaze the garlicky goodness from the bottom of the pan but realized I was out. With a shrug of my shoulders (and realizing that the pan was right at the sweet spot), I tilted my glass of red into the pan, and I've never looked back. Since butter and red wine make incredible accompaniments to steak, this broccoli preparation has become my default side when cooking Poole's Steak (page 217). **SERVES 4**

1 bunch broccoli (about 1 pound)

¼ cup neutral vegetable oil

2 cloves garlic, thinly sliced

Sea salt

½ cup red wine

3 tablespoons cold unsalted butter, cut into cubes

Black pepper in a mill

A generous squeeze of lemon juice

Trim the ends from the broccoli and discard or compost; cut the stems from the head. Slice the head into large florets. Peel the tough exterior of the stems, then halve them lengthwise and cut them into ¼-inch-thick half–moons. Set the broccoli pieces aside.

In a medium skillet over medium-high heat, heat the oil. When it shimmers, add the garlic and cook, stirring, for 20 seconds until it smells toasty and begins to curl. Add the broccoli and increase the heat to high. Season with ¼ teaspoon salt and cook, stirring occasionally to coat the broccoli, for about 2 minutes. Add the wine, bring to a boil, then reduce to a simmer. Let the liquid reduce by half, about 5 minutes.

Stir in the butter and continue to simmer for another 90 seconds, or until it's completely melted and combined. Remove from the heat. Season with 8 cranks of the pepper mill, salt to taste, and the lemon juice and serve immediately.

Roasted Carrots with Whipped Tahini

Carrots generally don't get the spotlight they deserve. Sure, they are called in to take supporting roles in soups, stocks, and salads. If and when the carrot is the star, little thought has been put into highlighting all of its attributes. It drives me crazy to see them overcooked or glazed in sugar.

The carrot is a diverse little garden beast, full of natural sweetness and a truly unique style of earthiness. Its skin is its most genuine connection to the soil in which it grows (I see you with that peeler in your hand . . . don't even think about it), and it's packed full of vitamins, minerals, and deliciousness. For this dish, I like to get an assortment of varieties and colors for the prettiest, most delicious final dish.

While overroasting is a common pitfall, roasting at too low a temperature is just as big a bummer. High heat is crucial to bring out the texture in the skin and allows the carrots to truly roast, yielding a well-cooked and slightly caramelized root that still has a good bite in the center.

This ramped-up version of tahini is a nutty complement to the sweet and earthy vibe of the carrots. **SERVES 6 to 8**

2 pounds medium carrots

1 tablespoon olive oil

Sea salt

Black pepper in a mill

5 medium thyme sprigs

1 fresh bay leaf

2 cloves garlic, crushed

2 tablespoons fresh orange juice

Zest from ½ orange

1 teaspoon toasted sesame oil

8 fresh mint leaves, torn

2 teaspoons toasted sesame or benne seeds

½ cup Whipped Tahini (page 62)

Preheat a convection oven to 400°F (or a regular oven to 425°F). Line a baking sheet with parchment.

Place the carrots in a large bowl with the olive oil, 1 teaspoon salt, about 20 turns of the pepper mill, thyme, bay, and garlic. Toss to coat well. Arrange the carrots on the parchment-lined baking sheet and bake for 20 minutes, rotating the pan 180 degrees halfway through. Let cool to room temperature.

Trim the ends of the carrots and cut on the diagonal into 2-inch-long pieces. Place in a medium bowl. Add the orange juice and zest, sesame oil, mint leaves, and sesame seeds and toss to coat. Spoon the tahini in the center of a serving platter. Arrange the carrots on top of the tahini and serve.

Duck Liver and Sweet Potato Dirty Rice Cakes

Dirty rice is a Creole dish in which rice is cooked with chicken livers and giblets (which darkens it to a "dirty" color), celery, peppers, onions, and, as I remember it from childhood, a goodly amount of rubbed sage. It earned a great deal of mainstream fame in my neck of the woods thanks to Bojangles, a local fried chicken chain that featured it as a side. (It's still my opinion that an extra-large half-cut Bojangles sweet tea is one of the best hangover cures in existence.)

In the Poole's version, we use duck livers. They are a bit richer, and just a little sweeter (also, we cook a lot of ducks, so we tend to stockpile the livers in our freezer). Dirty rice is such great way to make use of the spare parts of the duck (or chicken). The sweet potato adds texture and sweetness, while cooking the rice as a cake creates an opportunity for a crispy exterior and a creamy, tender center. We use rice grits, also called "middlins," which are broken bits that accumulate during the process of hulling the rice; they have a higher starch content, which yields an almost risotto-like end product. They're available online through Anson Mills; you can also use regular long-grain rice in this recipe.

This dish makes a great side, but it can truly stand on its own in the center of the plate. I like it with a simply dressed salad of spicy greens, like arugula or watercress. **SERVES 6 to 8**

¾ cup milk

4 ounces duck livers (or chicken livers), trimmed of sinews

Sea salt

Neutral vegetable oil

Kosher salt

¾ cup rice grits

1½ teaspoons unsalted butter

1 tablespoon flour

¼ cup heavy cream, warmed

1 tablespoon Dijon mustard

1 large egg

In a lidded container, submerge the livers in ½ cup milk and refrigerate for 8 hours or overnight. (This will pull out blood and impurities.) When ready to use, drain and rinse the livers, pat them dry, and season them lightly with sea salt.

Preheat a convection oven to 400°F (or a regular oven to 425°F).

In a medium skillet over medium heat, warm 2 teaspoons oil until it shimmers. Sear the livers until browned on each side, about 4 minutes total. The livers should still be pink in the center (you can cut one open to check). Transfer the livers to a plate to cool. When they're cool enough to handle, chop them finely and set aside.

Bring 4 cups water to a boil with 1 tablespoon kosher salt. Add the rice grits and stir. Cook for 7 to 9 minutes, stirring every couple of minutes, until the rice grits are just slightly al dente. Drain the rice grits and transfer to a shallow container to cool. Using your spoon, cut trails into the rice

½ cup finely grated raw sweet potato (using the small holes on a box grater)

2 tablespoons finely grated raw red onion (using the small holes on a box grater)

1 tablespoon chopped fresh sage

¾ cup finely grated Parmigiano-Reggiano

Black pepper in a mill

1 cup panko

grits to speed up the cooling and to prevent them from overcooking. (You may substitute 2½ cups cooked long-grain rice if you choose and skip this step all together.)

In a small skillet over low heat, melt the butter. When it's starting to froth, add the flour and stir constantly until the mixture comes together and begins to smell nutty, about 3 minutes. Add the remaining ¼ cup milk and the cream and stir until fully combined. Increase the heat to medium and bring to a simmer, then return the heat to low and cook, stirring, for 5 minutes. Remove this béchamel sauce from the heat and set aside.

When the rice grits are cool, transfer to a mixing bowl. Add the béchamel sauce, mustard, egg, sweet potato, red onion, sage, 2 teaspoons sea salt, the cheese, 15 cranks of the pepper mill, and the panko. Add the chopped livers and mix thoroughly by folding everything together with a rubber spatula. Taste for seasoning and add additional salt if needed.

Using a ½ cup measure, divide the batter into eight portions. Use your hands to mold each portion into a flat puck. Heat 2 tablespoons oil over medium-high heat in a large skillet. Once the oil is shimmering, add 4 cakes and sear, turning once. When both sides are golden brown and crispy, after about 6 minutes total, transfer to a baking sheet. Repeat this step with the remaining oil and rice cakes. Transfer the cakes to the oven and cook for 5 minutes to finish. Serve immediately.

Mashed Potatoes with Herb-Scented Cream

Most kids not-so-patiently wait to lick the beaters that are covered in cake batter; I preferred the ones that were coated in mashed potatoes. But I'm not alone in my preference: mashed potatoes are iconic, a long-standing American diner–menu staple. They make a creamy canvas for such comfort-food favorites as meatloaf, pork chops, and fried chicken, but I find them even dreamier planted next to stewed tomatoes and cornmeal-fried okra. Lumpy or smooth, and sometimes comprised of just enough potatoes to hold the butter and cream together, mashed potatoes are a guilty pleasure that makes us all feel warm, loved, and soulfully fed.

In this recipe, I scent the cream with aromatics that take the mashed potatoes from canvas to foreground—cream is an awesome vehicle for introducing flavors. Though gravy is always welcome, I think you'll find that these potatoes don't need it. **SERVES 6 to 8**

4 cups heavy cream

1½ teaspoons black peppercorns

½ shallot

1 head garlic, halved across the equator

1 fresh bay leaf

4 thyme sprigs

2 pounds Yukon gold potatoes

2 pounds russet potatoes

Kosher salt

1 cup unsalted butter, cut into cubes, at room temperature

Sea salt

In a large saucepan over medium heat, bring the cream, peppercorns, shallot, garlic, and bay leaf to a boil. Remove from the heat and add the thyme. Let steep for 15 minutes. Strain the cream through a fine-mesh sieve, discarding the solids and reserving the cream.

Peel the potatoes and cut them into 1-inch cubes. Place the potatoes in a pot with 10 cups water and season with 2 tablespoons kosher salt. Place the pot over high heat and bring to a boil. Reduce to a simmer and cook for 18 to 20 minutes, until the potatoes are fork-tender. Drain the potatoes well and return them to the pot.

In a large saucepan, warm the cream but don't let it boil. Place the pot of potatoes over low heat just to warm them through. Using an electric mixer, whip the potatoes on medium speed until smooth. Add half of the warm cream to the potatoes, followed by half of the butter. Continue to beat with the mixer, and when both are fully incorporated, continue to add the remaining cream and butter bit by bit until you've reached a silky-smooth consistency. You may not need all of the cream and butter; it depends on how starchy your potatoes are. Season the potatoes with 1 teaspoon sea salt or to taste and serve immediately.

Rose Finn Apple Potatoes with Shaved Celery, Buttermilk, and Dill

The first recipe I ever created was for potato salad. I was seven years old, and it was an assignment for our second-grade class. Though I had never made potato salad before, I was able to re-create the flavors and textures from the many versions I'd eaten at various cookouts. It's not that I had some highly evolved palate (because I didn't): I was able to recognize the different ingredients that make up the dish because most versions of potato salad lack unity. It makes it easy to pull apart the components—even for a seven-year-old.

The key to a well-rounded potato salad, in my opinion, is in the dressing: it has to be strong enough to flavor the potatoes to their core without overseasoning them. It's a balance that's nearly impossible to strike. The solution: poaching the potatoes in vinegar and salty water, which seasons the potatoes with the same flavors that appear in the dressing. Additionally, the vinegar helps preserve the texture of the potatoes, preventing you from accidentally cooking them to the point of no return.

In this recipe, I call for one of my favorite potatoes, the Rose Finn Apple. This potato has a tender reddish-beige skin and deep golden flesh. The flavor is sweet and buttery, as though a Yukon gold and a red new potato had a baby. You may of course sub in your favorite potato, but I promise it's worth snooping around to score the Rose Finn Apple.

SERVES 6 to 8

2½ pounds Rose Finn
    Apple potatoes

2 cups cider vinegar

¼ cup kosher salt

1 cup buttermilk

½ cup Countertop Crème Fraîche
    (page 159) or sour cream

½ cup Basic Cider Mayo
    (page 21)

2 tablespoons Dijon mustard

¼ cup finely chopped fresh dill

½ cup finely chopped green onions

Using a mandoline or a good sharp knife, slice the potatoes into ⅛-inch-thick coins. Rinse the potato slices in a colander, then place them in a large pot. Cover with 3 quarts water, the cider vinegar, and the kosher salt. Place the pot over high heat and bring to a boil. Reduce to a simmer and cook until the potatoes are just tender but not falling apart, 20 to 25 minutes. The skin of the potato should be fully intact, and the potato coins should hold their shape. Drain the potatoes (do not rinse them) and spread them out on a baking sheet; let cool to room temperature.

In a large mixing bowl, combine the buttermilk, crème fraîche, mayo, mustard, dill, green onions, salt, and shallot. Mix thoroughly.

Using a Microplane grater, zest the lemon over the dressing (this prevents losing any of the natural oil from the lemon), being careful not to

1 tablespoon sea salt

1 shallot, grated on a Microplane

1 lemon

2 cups paper-thin sliced celery (about 4 stalks)

Black pepper in a mill

zest any of the white pith, just the yellow peel. Stir in the celery, mixing to combine.

Add the potatoes to the bowl and stir with a spoon to coat the potatoes with the dressing. Because of the vinegar in their cooking liquid, the potato coins will maintain a snappy texture.

Season with a few cranks of the pepper mill, and let sit in the refrigerator for 1 hour before eating. The potato salad will keep in a lidded container in the refrigerator for up to 3 days, but taste and adjust for seasoning before serving as the flavors will change as they meld together.

I call this Homegrown Tomato Pie not as a sourcing requirement, but because the tomato pie is most present in the season where friends are pulling tomatoes daily from their own backyards. I imagine it came to be because, when a fruit is plentiful, people always find a way to bake it into a pie. Basil is a natural complement for this dish (and I've included it as an option), but the thyme is delicious and a bit unexpected. During the months when delicious tomatoes aren't flooding every backyard, our roasted Roma tomatoes sub in nicely (see page 162). I've made this a recipe for two pies, because in the event that you don't eat them both, gifting one to a friend or neighbor will earn you great favor.
MAKES two 9-inch pies

4 pounds tomatoes (beefsteak or heirloom are great; you could even use Romas)

Sea salt

2 large eggs

1½ cups Basic Cider Mayo (page 21)

2 tablespoons Dijon mustard

2 tablespoons prepared horseradish

¼ cup milk

¼ cup heavy cream

2 teaspoons chopped fresh thyme (or 12 fresh basil leaves, torn small)

1 pound buttermilk cheddar (extra-sharp cheddar is a suitable substitute), grated

Two 9-inch piecrust shells (see page 259), prebaked and cooled (see Note)

Black pepper in a mill

Continued

Preheat a convection oven to 350°F (or a regular oven to 375°F).

Fill a large pot three-quarters full with water and bring to a boil. While the water is coming up, core the tomatoes and, using a sharp knife, make a shallow X-shaped incision on the bottom of each, doing your best to cut just the skin and not into the flesh.

Once the water reaches a boil, prepare an ice bath by filling a large bowl with ice and water; set it within easy reach of the stove. Working in batches, place the tomatoes in the boiling water and cook until the cut skin at the bottom of the tomato begins to stretch and peel away; this usually takes between 45 and 90 seconds. As this happens, transfer the tomatoes one by one to the ice bath. Once the tomatoes are cool, peel their skins off using your hands and set them into a colander in the sink to drain off any excess liquid.

Slice the tomatoes into ¼-inch-thick slices and lay them out in a single layer on baking sheets. Generously season both sides of each tomato with sea salt (about twice as heavily as you would season a tomato to put in your sandwich). Allow the tomatoes to sit for 20 minutes. This will draw out moisture, which prevents the pie from being watery. Once the tomatoes have marinated for 20 minutes, transfer them to a salad spinner in three batches and spin the excess liquid off the tomatoes. (My mom taught me this trick; we like to save the drippings to make tomato vinaigrette or to throw into a vegetable sauté or pasta.)

note: I've made this recipe with store-bought frozen pie shells to great success. When going that route, I use what is referred to as deep-dish 9-inch frozen shells.

To make the custard, whisk the eggs in a mixing bowl. Whisk in the mayo, mustard, horseradish, milk, cream, and thyme.

Layer a small amount of the cheddar in the bottom of each piecrust, and then make a layer of tomato slices, with each slice's edge overlapping its neighbor's. Using the pepper grinder, crack peppercorns over the face of the tomatoes. Sprinkle on another layer of cheese, then drizzle enough of the custard over the top to drip through and cover all of the ingredients. Repeat these steps, starting with the tomatoes and ending with the custard, until all the ingredients are gone (I usually get three tomato layers). You'll need to bravely stack the ingredients just a bit higher than the edge of the piecrust. Have faith: it won't overflow.

Place the pies on baking sheets and transfer to the oven. Bake for 30 minutes, then rotate the pies 180 degrees and bake for another 30 minutes. Transfer to a cooling rack. Let cool and set for 1 hour before serving. Truth be told, if you can stand the wait, the pie is even better reheated the next day. Reheat the pies in a 350°F convection oven (375°F regular) until warm throughout, about 20 minutes.

Latkes with Crème Fraîche

I didn't grow up eating latkes. I ate my first one as an adult, but the flavors and textures were immediately recognizable to me as an elevated form of something that every Waffle House and nearly every greasy spoon has in abundance: hash browns.

As Poole's has evolved, our definition of comfort food has broadened to be something that transcends cultural borders. Latkes have the flavor landmarks of a universal dish, but what really makes them fit on the menu at Poole's is that they are a humble food associated with celebration.

For my latke recipe, I finely grate the onion on the small side of a Microplane grater, which uniformly incorporates the flavor of onion throughout the latke, eliminating any out-of-balance bites. It also creates a more uniform exterior as the sugar in the onions tends to darken before the potatoes do.

Tangy Countertop Crème Fraîche is a must with a proper latke. Other worthy accoutrements include chives, smoked fish, caviar, pickled red cabbage, and even braised apples. **SERVES 8**

1 pound russet potatoes
(2 or 3 medium potatoes)

1 large egg, beaten

6 tablespoons oat flour
(or all-purpose flour)

1 tablespoon finely grated
yellow onion

1½ teaspoons sea salt

⅓ cup neutral vegetable oil,
plus more for frying

1 tablespoon unsalted butter

Countertop Crème Fraîche
(page 159), for serving

Preheat a convection oven to 350°F (or a regular oven to 375°F). Using a mandoline outfitted with a fine julienne blade, carefully cut the potatoes lengthwise. Place in a colander set inside a large bowl in the sink and rinse under cold running water for 15 minutes, agitating every few minutes to help remove the starch. Spin the potatoes dry in a salad spinner.

In a large mixing bowl, combine the potatoes, egg, flour, onion, and salt. Mix well with your hands.

Place a large oven-safe skillet over high heat and add the oil. (Use a lightweight pan, which will be easier to flip.) When the skillet is very hot, add the latke batter and use a spatula to spread it out into an even cake about 1 inch thick. Let cook for about 6 minutes, running a spatula around the edge of the pan frequently and gently pushing the edges of the potato inward to form a nice edge.

Lift the pan and shimmy the cake toward the far lip of the pan; slip the spatula under the cake and quickly and confidently flip the cake. Cook for 2 minutes more, then slip the butter under the edge of the cake. Transfer the skillet to the oven and bake for 10 minutes. Turn out onto a cutting board, cut into slices, and serve with dollops of crème fraîche.

Countertop Crème Fraîche

Cultured dairy is being embraced in mainstream cooking right now, and if you're reading this book in fifty years, I hope this continues to be the case. From Greek yogurt to *labne*, buttermilk to crème fraîche, the richness and tang of this family of ingredients is a huge boon to a cook.

If you've never experimented with making cheese or butter, this recipe is a great first step. Crème fraîche is really no more than a combo of heavy cream and buttermilk. Leave the mixture on your counter for 2 to 3 days (covered with cheesecloth), and the cultures react to thicken into an amazing, completely new ingredient. It's especially worth doing if you have access to really good buttermilk or heavy cream. Next time you're close to a high-quality dairy farm (or their farmers' market stand), grab the goods to try this recipe. You'll never go back to store-bought crème fraîche. (However, if you are purchasing crème fraîche or sour cream, go with an all-natural option, free of stabilizers.)

I love using this to make beluga lentils more luxe, or scenting it with horseradish and using it on top of a baked potato. **MAKES 2½ cups**

2 cups heavy cream
½ cup buttermilk

Mix the ingredients in a mason jar. Cover the top with a square of cheese-cloth and secure with a rubber band or twine. Let sit on the counter for 2 to 3 days, or until thickened. Transfer to lidded containers and store in the refrigerator for up to 2 weeks.

Vidalia Onion Rings

I can spot a bad onion ring from a mile away. It's perfectly battered, as though the coating was hand-painted. You can't see any of the onion peering through, and the rings themselves look like they were spun off of a band saw. My point? If any onion ring looks *too* perfect, be suspicious.

The best onion rings are imperfect. They barely hold on to their simple batter of seasoned flour and cornstarch, bound by a splash of good buttermilk. The slightly mismatched size of the rings (a product of free-handed knife cuts) allows the batter to bind in different thicknesses and produces striations of crunch and crisp. The bits of coating that break away in the fryer should reveal stained glass–like panes of caramelized onion through the broken batter shell.

These make a great starter at a gathering where bare hands, a roll of paper towels, and a cooler of cold beer would not be out of place, but we usually serve them on the table as a side dish. Dig in and consider a bib for the shrapnel blanket of crispy bits. **SERVES 6 to 8**

4 Vidalia or other sweet onions

3 cups all-purpose flour

1 cup cornstarch

2 tablespoons sea salt

1 tablespoon freshly ground
    black pepper

Neutral vegetable oil, for frying

Trim the tip and tail of each onion, then cut the onions into fat, ¾- to 1-inch-thick rings crosswise (across the equator). Break the onion slices up into their natural rings, discarding the centers.

Mix the flour, cornstarch, salt, and pepper in a large bowl. Line a baking sheet with two or three layers of paper towels. Fill a heavy-bottomed pot or Dutch oven with 3 to 4 inches of oil and set over high heat until the oil reaches 350°F on a deep-fry thermometer. Dredge the onion rings in the flour mixture, coating them well. Transfer them in batches to the pot and fry until golden brown, flipping occasionally, 5 to 6 minutes. Transfer to the prepared baking sheet and season with sea salt. Serve with your choice of condiment (I'm a fan of the Basic Malt Mayo on page 21).

Roasted Tomatoes

As a tomato addict, I can't imagine waiting through all of the cold months without tomatoes, longing for the first local vines to fruit. This is my solution: I can find a semidecent Roma tomato in almost any city in any month, and roasting them makes the most of their flavor even in the cold season. It reduces their water content and intensifies the fruit flavor, coaxing out vibrancy you could never detect in their raw state. Roasted tomato has the perfect balance of sweetness and acidity, characteristics that put it up there with lemons as far as versatility goes. If you like, add garlic, thyme, or minced shallots to flavor the tomatoes while they cook. Roasted tomato BLTs are a staff meal favorite at Poole's. **MAKES about 3 cups**

3 pounds Roma tomatoes, halved lengthwise

¼ cup olive oil

Sea salt

Preheat a convection oven to 300°F (or a regular oven to 325°F). Line two baking sheets with parchment paper.

In a large bowl, toss the tomato halves with the olive oil, then place cut side up on the prepared baking sheets. Season generously with sea salt.

Transfer to the oven and roast for 2 hours, or until the flesh of the tomatoes has shriveled and their volume has reduced slightly. Flip the tomatoes over, cut side down, and roast for 30 more minutes.

Let the tomatoes cool for 30 minutes. While the tomatoes are still slightly warm, pull the skins off using your hands.

You can store roasted tomatoes, covered with olive oil, in a mason jar for up to 1 month in the fridge. Otherwise, they'll keep for about 1 week in the fridge. You can also freeze the tomatoes in a resealable plastic bag (try to remove as much air from the bag as possible before sealing) for up to 3 months.

note: For Roasted Tomato Relish, combine 1 cup chopped Roasted Tomatoes, 1 tablespoon minced shallots, and 2 or 3 cranks of black pepper from a pepper mill in a medium bowl. Drizzle with 2 tablespoons extra-virgin olive oil and fold to combine. Makes about 1 cup.

Malted Slaw with Roasted Tomatoes

There are plenty of roadside- and buffet-style dishes that I carry a torch for in a serious way. Slaw isn't one of them.

I think bad slaw is one of the reasons mayonnaise gets a bad rap. The type of slaw I'm speaking of has an unappealing sweetness and a soggy texture; the dressing pools on your plate rather than clinging eagerly to the cabbage. If any of these characteristics have kept you from embracing slaw in the past, I'm hoping this will be the recipe that brings you into the fold.

The answer isn't in changing up the ingredients: this slaw features the classic combo of cabbage and mayonnaise. But giving a vinegary backbone to the mayo and soaking the cabbage in an ice brine give this version an acidic, crunchy edge. Roasted Tomatoes, our back pocket workhorse, bring a sweetness into the mix and round out the malt in the mayo. **SERVES 6 to 8**

½ head green cabbage
(about 1¼ pounds)

¼ cup kosher salt

4 cups ice

12 roasted tomato halves
(see page 162), quartered

9 green onions, trimmed and
thinly sliced on the diagonal

2 teaspoons freshly ground
black pepper

2 teaspoons sea salt

1 teaspoon celery seed, toasted

Zest of ½ lemon

1 teaspoon Dijon mustard

¾ cup Basic Malt Mayo
(page 21)

Cut the cabbage into quarters and remove the core. Using a mandoline, very thinly slice the cabbage into ribbons. In a large bowl, combine 2 quarts water and the kosher salt; stir until the salt dissolves, then add the ice. Add the cabbage and soak for 20 minutes; drain very well. Use a salad spinner to remove any residual liquid from the cabbage. Place the cabbage in a bowl with the tomato halves and the green onions. Set aside.

In a second bowl, combine the pepper, sea salt, celery seed, lemon, mustard, and mayo. Pour the mayo mixture over the cabbage mixture and stir until everything is well coated and combined. Serve immediately.

Bowls & Such

There's a specific posture we generally revert to when eating a dish out of a bowl. We curve over with rounded back to meet it, getting our face as close as possible to what lies within. Bowls, with their curved edges and slurp-worthy contents, have a magnetic pull.

This type of body language is particularly noticeable at the bar at Poole's. It's pretty easy to spot who is halfway through a bowl of Macaroni au Gratin (page 190) versus a beet salad—just look for the curled-over back.

If Poole's is a meditation on comfort food, then these are the dishes that hew most closely to a standard definition of the term; they conjure warmth, they make the pleasure receptors fire, and they incite feelings of satisfaction. They're hearty, rich, and unapologetic.

Many of them require time to come together, and when they do, they're fully formed, without any need for an accompanying side dish or share plate. Bowls tread the line between the communal and the solitary, comprising soups and stews that can feed many but served in a style that focuses on the individual.

Whether it's a bowl of risotto-style broken rice or a riff on chicken and dumplings, these recipes soothe as much as they satiate.

Chilled Corn Soup with Cherry Tomatoes

I never get tired of watching friends eat this soup for the first time. They take a bite and rather than a thick, creamy puree, the soup in their mouths has the texture of clouds . . . delicious corn-flavored clouds.

In the restaurant, we achieve this pillowy consistency through the use of an iSi cream whipper (those contraptions you see baristas using to pile whipped cream on iced mochas). These are readily available on Amazon and at kitchen stores like Williams-Sonoma, should you want to invest in one. It makes a great party trick. But you can also whip the soup with an electric mixer to almost the same effect. **SERVES 6 to 8**

CORN STOCK

6 ears corn, shucked, kernels removed and reserved, and cobs reserved

CORN CREAM

3 cups corn kernels, reserved from making the stock

3 cups heavy cream

Sea salt

CORN RELISH

1 cup slivered cherry tomatoes

Sea salt

1 cup corn kernels (from about 2 ears of corn)

2 tablespoons minced shallot

2 tablespoons chopped fresh parsley or basil

1 tablespoon chopped fresh chives, in ¼-inch pieces

¼ cup olive oil

Flaky sea salt (such as Maldon)

note: Whipping in a stand mixer requires the mix to be creamier to achieve the correct volume, so there's no need to add additional stock.

To make the stock, snap the corncobs in half, place in a large stockpot, and add enough water to cover by 1 inch. Bring to a gentle boil and cook for 1 hour. Strain the stock through a fine-mesh sieve and let cool to room temperature. Store in lidded containers in the refrigerator until ready to use. (The stock can be made 2 days in advance.)

To make the corn cream, combine the corn kernels and cream in a heavy saucepan over medium-high heat and bring to a boil. Reduce the heat to low and let simmer for 30 minutes. Using an immersion blender or a stand blender, puree the mixture plus 1 cup of the reserved corn stock well (if using a stand blender, work in batches and fill the blender only half full, leaving a gap in the lid for steam to vent). Strain the puree through a very fine-mesh sieve set over a large bowl, and season with 1 teaspoon of salt. Let cool completely, then transfer to a lidded container and refrigerate until ready to use. (The cream can be made 1 day in advance.)

To make the relish, place the tomatoes in a small bowl, and season with ½ teaspoon of salt. Let sit for 7 minutes, then add the corn kernels, shallot, parsley, chives, and oil and stir to combine.

If using an iSi whipper, combine the corn cream and 1 cup of the reserved stock. Pour 2 cups of the mixture into the iSi canister, close tightly, and charge with 2 charges. Dispense the soup into bowls and top with spoonfuls of the relish. Repeat in batches with the remaining soup base and relish. Garnish all bowls with coarse sea salt and serve.

If using a stand mixer, place the corn cream (without additional stock; see Note) into the bowl of the mixer fitted with a whisk attachment; whip until the consistency of whipped cream. Follow the serving instructions.

Cauliflower Soup with Sultanas and Crispy Capers

It's frequently a point of discussion that chefs don't cook much at home. While it's true that working service every night means that you're rarely home to cook dinner, I've still always carved out time to cook at home on my days off. My favorite thing to make? Soup. It's an easygoing, even meditative process that sets you up with meals for the week ahead. Plus, it's the kind of activity that easily allows for breaks to read the paper, catch up on chores, etcetera.

This recipe is a ringer from one such day off. Steaming the cauliflower with the onion develops a rich, dynamic flavor, while emulsifying the soup base with butter at the end of cooking creates richness. **SERVES 4**

2 tablespoons neutral vegetable oil

1 large yellow onion, thinly sliced

1 head cauliflower, washed and cut into florets

2 cups heavy cream

4 tablespoons cold unsalted butter, cut into cubes

Sea salt

CRISPY CAPERS

¼ cup capers, drained

½ cup neutral vegetable oil

SULTANA RELISH

¼ cup sultanas

½ cup boiling water

1 tablespoon minced shallot

1 tablespoon olive oil

To make the soup, place a saucepan over medium heat. Add the oil, and when it shimmers, add the onion. Stirring with a wooden spoon, cook the onion until tender, about 7 minutes. Add the cauliflower, season lightly with salt, and stir to coat with the onion and oil. Add a splash of water, cover, and steam until tender, about 8 minutes.

Uncover and add the cream and enough water to just cover the cauliflower. Simmer until the cauliflower is tender to the point of falling apart, 15 to 20 minutes. Using an immersion blender or a stand blender, puree until airy and smooth. Season the puree with salt to taste. Add the butter 1 tablespoon at a time, and puree after each addition.

To make the crispy capers, place the capers and oil in a small saucepan and set over medium heat. Let the oil heat up; the capers will begin to fry. Once the capers are bubbling, cook for 1 minute, then use a fine-mesh sieve to transfer the capers to a paper towel–lined plate. Reserve.

To make the sultana relish, in a small bowl, combine the sultanas and the boiling water. Let sit until the water is room temperature. Drain the sultanas, coarsely chop, and place in a bowl. Stir in the shallot and olive oil. Set aside until ready to use.

To serve, reheat the soup gently, ladle into bowls, and garnish with a spoonful each of the relish and the capers.

Mussels with White Wine and Dijon

For me, freshly harvested mussels simply prepared fall in the category of *wonder food*. You start with a handful of ingredients and end up with a dish more complex than the time and resources invested. Mussels are givers: when cooked, they create a fresh broth that is as rich and rounded as something that has been simmering for days.

I love to match the sweet meat and brine of the mollusk with the sharpness of my favorite French Dijon mustard, Edmond Fallot. A touch of cream grounds these brilliant flavors, while the lemon lifts them up so that our taste buds can afford to down a whole bowl without getting weighed down by the richness.

This dish is a tribute to the king of all mussels, who "flexes" them more graciously than anyone I've ever known: my brother from another mother, chef Matthew Kelly. Thanks for the gift of your friendship and for all of the shared meals. **SERVES 4**

2 tablespoons neutral vegetable oil

2 large shallots, thinly sliced and broken up into rings (about 3½ ounces)

4 thyme sprigs

2 cloves garlic, smashed

Sea salt

2 pounds mussels, scrubbed and beards removed (see page 174)

1 cup dry white wine

2 tablespoons Dijon mustard

1 cup heavy cream

3 tablespoons cold unsalted butter, cut into cubes

Juice of 1 lemon

4 thick slices baguette, toasted

1 tablespoon lemon zest, for garnish (optional)

Continued

In a large Dutch oven over medium heat, heat the oil and swirl to coat the pan. When the oil shimmers, add the shallots, thyme, garlic, and ½ teaspoon salt and cook, stirring frequently, until the shallots begin to caramelize slightly, about 4 minutes. Add the mussels and stir well to coat in the oil, then continue stirring for about 1 minute to toast the mussels in their shells. Stir in the wine, cover, and cook for 3 minutes. Place a bowl next to the stove.

Uncover the pan and use tongs to transfer the cooked mussels from the pan to the bowl; you'll know they are done when the shells have opened, the meat inside the shells is pulling away from the walls of the shell, and the center of the meat no longer looks creamy. Some mussels will reach this point 1 minute after uncovering the pan, while others might take to 4 or 5 minutes. Take your time and fish the mussels out only when they've reached that perfect state of doneness. Discard any mussels that haven't opened after 8 minutes.

Leave the white wine liquid in the pan and increase the heat to high. Whisk the mustard into the liquid and let simmer for 1 minute. Whisk in the cream. When the mixture comes to a boil, add the butter and swirl the pan to help distribute it evenly. When the butter has melted, return the return the mussels to the pan and reheat, stirring constantly, for 1 minute.

Remove from the heat and squeeze the lemon juice over the mussels; stir once more to incorporate.

To serve, place 1 baguette slice in the bottom of each of four bowls and divide the mussels and cream among the bowls. Alternatively, you can serve this family style, as we do, in a big serving bowl with the bread on the side. Encourage your guests to dip the bread directly into the bowl for proper soppage.

| ABOUT MUSSELS |

Everyone has a "bad shellfish" story. Mussels are frequently the culprits in these stories, but it doesn't have to be that way. A bad mussel is easy to avoid if you know how to spot it. First things first: buy the freshest live mussels you can find, from a reputable seafood source.

Then, check their vitals:

- Before you cook your mussels, take a look and separate any that are slightly open. Give these open ones a gentle tap on your counter. If they close, the mussel is alive and good to go; if it stays open, it's dead. Say your good-byes and toss it.

- Smell your mussels: live, fresh mussels will smell of the sea, but this won't be an overpowering scent. Only dead or past-their-prime mussels will give off that murky, low-tide funk that we associate with certain shellfish.

- When you cook your mussels, you might have one or two that don't open when exposed to heat. Pull these from your pot and throw them out.

| CLEANING MUSSELS |

Cleaning mussels is much easier than most people think. Really all they need is a rinse and a shave. (While in the water, mussels affix to surfaces with thin, stringy membranes commonly called "beards." These need to be removed before cooking.)

First, place your (good-smelling, alert) mussels in a colander and rinse well with cold water. Use a paper towel to rub off any mud or seaweed. With your fingers or a pair of needle-nose pliers, pull any thin strands of "beard" firmly downward toward the hinged side of the mussel until the strand releases.

Oyster Stew with Twice-Fried Saltines and Charred Turnip Relish

The secret to this rich, indulgent stew is only partially in the cream. Oysters are pureed into the base, which connects their briny salinity to the rest of the ingredients and naturally thickens the soup. It builds an undeniably oystery backbone. The turnips provide a sharp, wasabi-like heat that brings the luxurious richness of the soup back into balance. I've always loved the oyster crackers that come alongside a bowl of chowder. The fried saltines operate along the same principle, but are even more delicious. **SERVES 8**

CHARRED TURNIP RELISH

1 tablespoon neutral vegetable oil

4 ounces turnip greens

Sea salt

1 tablespoon minced shallot

Zest of ½ lemon

¾ cup extra virgin olive oil

OYSTER STEW

3 cups shucked oysters in their liquid (about 30 oysters)

2 tablespoons neutral vegetable oil

2 cups thinly sliced yellow onions (about 1 medium onion)

2 cups thinly sliced fennel (about 1 bulb)

2 cups diced turnip (about 2 small turnips)

2 cloves garlic, crushed

A large sachet (see page 18)

1 tablespoon sea salt

1 cup white wine

1 cup dry vermouth

6 cups heavy cream

1 cup Dijon mustard

TWICE-FRIED SALTINES

Neutral vegetable oil, for frying

1 sleeve saltines

To make the relish, add the oil to a large cast-iron skillet over medium heat. When it's hot, add the greens and cook, flipping the leaves occasionally, until they have a nice sear on them, about 3 minutes. Season with salt and transfer to a cutting board or baking sheet to cool. Once cool, finely chop the greens and place in a medium bowl. Fold in the shallot and lemon zest, then mix in the olive oil. Refrigerate until ready to use.

Place the oysters in a fine-mesh sieve set over a bowl and drain well.

Place a large saucepot or Dutch oven over medium heat and add the oil. Once the oil is shimmering, add the onions, fennel, turnip, and garlic. Reduce the heat and sweat until tender, about 8 minutes. Add the sachet and salt. Stir until you can smell the herbs in the sachet.

Add the white wine and vermouth and bring the mixture to a boil. Lower to a simmer and reduce the liquid by half. Add 1 cup of the drained oysters, the juice that has collected in the bowl, the cream, and the mustard. Bring to a simmer and let simmer for 10 minutes. Discard the sachet.

While the stew is simmering, make the saltines. Line a plate with paper towels. Heat ½ inch of oil in a skillet over high heat. When the oil reaches 325°F on a deep-fry thermometer, add the saltines in batches of 6 crackers and fry, turning frequently, for 1 to 2 minutes, until tanned. Transfer to the plate and reserve.

Using an immersion blender or food processor, puree the stew mixture until smooth. Strain through a fine-mesh sieve and return the liquid to the pot. (You can prepare the stew up to this step up to 1 day before.) Place over medium heat; add the remaining drained oysters and stir, cooking for just 1 or 2 minutes more to warm the oysters. Ladle into bowls and serve with the twice-fried saltines broken up over the top and a dollop of relish.

Caramelized Onion–Tomato Soup with Jarlsberg Croutons

This recipe combines two of the most comforting soups in existence—tomato soup and French onion soup—into one powerhouse of a bowl. The key to nailing this dish is patience: each step, from slowly caramelizing the onions to reducing the tarragon stock, takes time. You'll be rewarded on the other side with a rich and complex flavor with the heft of beef stock, even though the soup is entirely vegetarian.

The soup is great on its own, but the addition of melty Jarlsberg cheese and toasted baguette makes it worthy of a special occasion (or a proper rainy day). **SERVES 6**

½ cup olive oil

6 cloves garlic, crushed

2 (28-ounce) cans diced
    organic tomatoes

Sea salt

2 tablespoons neutral vegetable oil

2 pounds yellow onions, halved and
    thinly sliced (about 6 cups)

4 cups dry white wine

¼ cup white wine vinegar

6 to 7 whole sprigs tarragon,
    leaves intact

1 tablespoon whole-grain mustard

CROUTONS

1 tablespoon neutral vegetable oil

½ baguette, sliced into
    ¼-inch-thick slices

1 tablespoon unsalted butter

½ cup grated Jarlsberg (any nutty,
    melty cheese, such as Gruyère,
    would work well here)

In a large Dutch oven, combine the olive oil and garlic. Place over medium heat and cook, stirring occasionally, until the garlic is toasted, about 2 minutes. Add the tomatoes and 2 teaspoons sea salt and increase the heat to bring to a boil. Reduce to a simmer. Cook for 45 minutes; the tomatoes and garlic will be falling apart and the flavors will be cohesive.

Meanwhile, in a high-sided sauté pan, heat the vegetable oil over medium heat. Add the onions and 2 teaspoons salt. Turn the heat to high, stirring frequently. Once the pan is hot (about 1 minute), reduce the heat to medium and cover; cook, covered, for 20 minutes. When you remove the lid, lots of moisture will escape, and the onions will have begun to caramelize. Cook, stirring, until the onions are thick and deep brown. Transfer the onions to a bowl and return the pan to high heat.

Add the wine, vinegar, and tarragon. Cook until the liquid has reduced down to become thick and syrupy. Add 6 cups water and bring to a boil, then remove from the heat.

Strain the tarragon infusion into the stewed tomato mixture, discarding the solids. Stir in the caramelized onions, mustard, and 2 teaspoons salt. Bring the soup to a boil, then reduce to a simmer and let simmer for 20 minutes.

While the soup is simmering, make the croutons. Line a plate with paper towels. In a large skillet over high heat, heat the oil. When it shimmers, add the baguette slices in an even layer; when they begin to turn golden on the bottom side, add the butter, turn down the heat to medium, and swirl to coat. Fry the bread for 3 to 4 minutes on one side, until it is a dark golden brown. Transfer to the paper towel–lined plate.

Continued

Stack three croutons in the center of each of six ovenproof soup bowls, placing a small pinch of cheese between each layer. Ladle the soup around the stacks of bread to fill the bowls. Sprinkle a last pinch of cheese in the center of each bowl. Place the bowls under the broiler and cook for 2 to 3 minutes, until the cheese is melted and bubbling. Serve.

Creamy Rice Grits

I didn't go to culinary school, but I have had many teachers, starting with my family. Later, as I dove deeper into cooking as a career, I looked to cookbooks like Paul Bertolli's *Cooking by Hand* and Tom Colicchio's *Think Like a Chef*. From these pages (and a list of others too long to print), I learned about the techniques and classic dishes of French and Italian kitchens, which I eagerly incorporated into my own cooking repertoire. At the time they felt new and exciting and fancy compared to the food I knew by heart.

These days, some of my favorite new discoveries come from the farmers and growers that provide Poole's with ingredients. Glenn Roberts of Anson Mills is one such teacher—a true wealth of knowledge on the grains of the South. He introduced me to rice grits (traditionally known as "shorts" or "middlins"), a short, very absorbent grain that I absolutely love. The grits are actually a by-product of milling Carolina Gold rice, which is highly fragile and frequently breaks. These broken pieces become rice grits; because of the break in the grain, they release more starch than most rice.

The first time I tried them, I couldn't believe how similar they were to Arborio, the rice variety traditionally used in risotto. Suddenly those cookbook recipes I cooked early in my career had come full circle, through an ingredient from close to home. **SERVES 8**

2¼ cups Carolina Gold rice grits

Kosher salt

1 cup finely grated Parmesan

4 tablespoons unsalted butter

3 tablespoons fresh lemon juice

3 tablespoons extra-virgin olive oil

Sea salt

Black pepper in a mill

Bring 3 quarts water to a boil in a large saucepan. Stir in the grits and season with 2 tablespoons kosher salt. Reduce the heat to medium and simmer the grits until almost tender, 5 to 6 minutes. Drain, reserving 2 cups of the cooking liquid; return the liquid and the grits to the saucepan. Stir over medium heat until creamy, 5 to 6 minutes. Add the cheese and butter and stir to melt. Stir in the lemon juice and olive oil and season with sea salt and pepper. Serve immediately.

Yukon Gold Potato Soup with Buttermilk and Bacon

When it comes to comfort food, baked potatoes are at the very top of my list. I'm pretty sure it's a not-so-secret craving for most chefs. This soup is an homage to that affection.

You'll note that the potatoes get a long rinse before heading into the pot. Don't skip this step: it rids the potatoes of excess starch, which keeps the soup from being gummy.

This can be easily adapted for vegetarians and vegans; simply omit the buttermilk and the bacon garnish. **SERVES 8 to 10**

2 pounds Yukon gold potatoes, peeled and cut into ¼-inch-thick rounds

2 tablespoons neutral vegetable oil

1 celery stalk, thinly sliced

2 leeks, halved and sliced into half-moons (about 1½ cups)

1 large shallot, thinly sliced (about ½ cup)

A large sachet (see page 18)

Sea salt

½ cup dry white wine

12 ounces bacon slices

2 cups buttermilk, at room temperature

3 green onions, thinly sliced

Black pepper in a mill

Place the potatoes in a colander and set it in a large bowl in the sink. Run the potatoes under a small, steady stream of water for 15 minutes, changing the water captured in the bowl every 5 minutes to remove any starch that's settled to the bottom. Drain the potatoes and set aside.

In a large Dutch oven, heat the oil over medium heat. When it shimmers, add the celery, leeks, shallot, and sachet. Stir to coat evenly with the oil, then cover and cook for 4 minutes, until the vegetables are softened. Stir in ¼ teaspoon salt and the wine, increase the heat to high, and reduce until the wine is almost evaporated.

Stir in the potatoes, coating them in the onion mixture. Add 2 quarts water and 2 teaspoons of salt and bring to a boil. Reduce to a simmer and cook for 30 minutes, or until the potatoes are starting to fall apart.

Preheat a convection oven to 350°F (or a regular oven to 375°F). Line a baking sheet with foil and arrange the bacon strips on it in a single layer. Bake for 20 minutes, or until crispy and dark brown. Pour the bacon fat off into a heatproof bowl and reserve; when the bacon is cool enough to handle, roughly chop and set aside.

Remove the soup from the heat and discard the sachet. Using an immersion blender or stand blender, puree the soup until smooth (if using a stand blender, fill only half full and leave a gap in the lid for steam to vent). Do not overmix. Return the puree to the pan, whisk in the buttermilk, and season with salt.

To serve, place 2 teaspoons of the reserved bacon fat in a small skillet over medium heat. Add the bacon bits and toss for 30 seconds to coat. Ladle the soup into bowls and garnish with some of the green onions, a teaspoon of bacon bits and fat, and a few cranks of the pepper mill.

Duck Slick

One of the most fulfilling aspects of running Poole's Diner has been continuously crossing paths with folks who were dedicated patrons way back when it was John Poole's original luncheonette. I love hearing about morning streak o' lean (a dish of boiled and fried pork fatback) and lunchtime blue-plate pot roast, but the dish that casts the largest shadow is chicken slick: a rich plate of chicken in white gravy, with slick, fat noodles made from a dough spiked with schmaltz. Other dialects refer to this as chicken and dumplings or chicken and pastry, but here we call it slick. (The origins of the name are debated: some say that "slick" is specific to a dumpling made without baking powder, while others say that "slick" is an adjective describing the dough when made correctly.) It is an essential player in the Southern diner game. Our version bats by the same rules, but with rich duck confit in place of simmered chicken and, naturally, with unctuous duck fat in the ribbon-like noodles. **SERVES 4**

NOODLES

½ pound all-purpose flour

Sea salt

2 large eggs

3 tablespoons rendered duck fat

SLICK

1½ quarts Rich Poultry Stock (page 24)

1 teaspoon sea salt

3 tablespoons cold Roasted Garlic Butter (page 20), cut into cubes

2 cups pulled duck confit (see page 38)

2 scallions, greens only, thinly sliced

Black pepper in a mill

Continued

To make the noodles, in the bowl of a stand mixer fitted with the dough hook, combine the flour and ¾ teaspoon salt. In a separate bowl, using a fork, mix the eggs, duck fat, and 3 tablespoons of water. With the mixer on low speed, slowly drizzle the egg mixture into the flour mixture. The dough should come together into a ball. Transfer the ball from the mixer to a floured work surface and knead until smooth (6 to 8 minutes). Wrap the dough tightly in plastic wrap, and let it rest for at least 1 hour (and up to 1 day) in the refrigerator.

Divide the dough into two equal pieces. Using a rolling pin or a pasta machine, roll the dough very thin to about ¹⁄₁₆ inch thickness. Using a pasta cutter or a sharp knife, cut the rolled dough into 1-inch-wide by 4-inch-long strips. Let some of the strips be imperfect on the ends and some of the edges, making use of all of the dough. Lay the noodles out on a flat surface. (Or, if you're making them in advance, transfer to a baking sheet and freeze until ready to use. The noodles can be frozen for up to 1 month.)

To make the slick, in a large pot over high heat, bring the poultry stock to a boil. Season with the salt. Add the noodles to the stock one by one so they don't clump or stick. Once all of the noodles are in the pot, return the pot to a boil and cook, stirring occasionally, for 14 minutes; the noodles will absorb some of the stock, and the starch will create a gravy-like sauce. Reduce the heat to low, add the garlic butter and swirl the pan until the butter has melted and emulsified into the sauce. Fold in the duck confit and cook to warm through. Taste and season with salt to your preference and 20 cranks of the pepper mill. Top with the sliced scallions and serve.

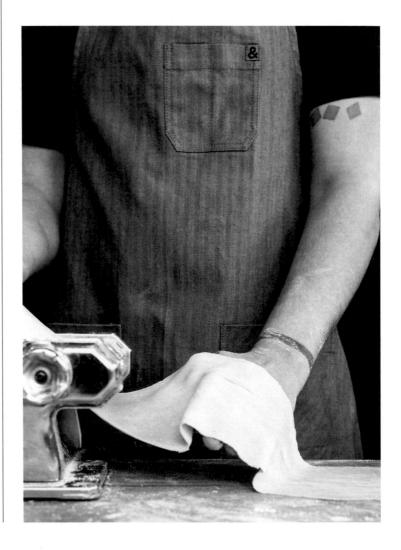

Pork and Dumplings with Stewed Tomatoes and Butter Beans

Yes, this is one of those annoying recipes that plagues cookbooks, requiring multiple components and subrecipes. It's a project, and it's important to know that going in. But I can think of no nicer way to spend a Sunday afternoon than braising some pork shanks and rolling out some dumplings. And trust me when I say that there's no nicer reward than sitting down with a group of friends to dig into the final dish. These dumplings are technically *gnudi*, the ricotta-based version of Italian gnocchi. If you don't want to go to all the trouble of making the other components, you could toss the dumplings with some tomato sauce and be in great shape for dinner. We've also used them as the base of a dish with shredded short-rib meat (see page 213), fried slivered onions, and horseradish.

But don't be deterred from making this all the way through, at least once. You can make all of the pieces—stewed tomatoes, butter beans, dumplings, and pork—ahead of time, and the whole thing comes together in less than 10 minutes. (Break it out at a dinner party and you'll look like a pro.) **SERVES 6 to 8**

DUMPLINGS

3¼ cups whole-milk ricotta cheese

3 large egg yolks

1 whole large egg

1½ teaspoons sea salt

1 cup plus 1 tablespoon 00 flour, plus more for dusting

2 tablespoons neutral vegetable oil

1 cup fresh butter beans

Kosher salt

A small sachet (page 18)

3 cups Stewed Tomatoes (page 142)

2 cups braised pork shank meat, plus ½ cup pork cooking liquid (page 246)

To make the dumplings, in a large bowl, mix together the ricotta, egg yolks, whole egg, and sea salt until well blended. Pass the mixture through a fine-mesh sieve, and return to a large mixing bowl. Add the flour, mix well, and transfer to a pastry bag fitted with ¾-inch round tip.

Bring a large pot of heavily salted water (it should taste salty like the sea) to a boil. On a heavily floured surface pipe the mixture out in 8-inch-long lines. Use a bench scraper or your hands to carefully roll the rows back and forth in the flour to coat.

With a sharp knife, cut the rows of dough into 1-inch pieces. Add the pieces to the boiling water a few at a time (so they don't stick) and cook until the dough is just cooked through (about 3 minutes). Remove from the water with a slotted spoon and transfer to a paper towel–lined baking sheet to cool. When all of the dumplings have been cooked, transfer to a bowl and drizzle with the vegetable oil; toss to coat. Set aside. (The dumplings can be made up to 2 days in advance and stored in a lidded container in the refrigerator.)

2 tablespoons cold Roasted Garlic Butter (page 20), cut into cubes

2 tablespoons cold unsalted butter, cut into cubes

Juice of ½ lemon

Finely grated Parmigiano-Reggiano, for serving

Rinse the beans, place in a saucepan, and cover with 2 cups cool water. Bring to boil over high heat, then reduce to a simmer and cook until tender, 25 to 30 minutes. The beans should still hold their shape but be tender throughout. Stir in 1½ teaspoons kosher salt, add the sachet, and remove from the heat. Allow the beans to cool to room temperature in the cooking liquid. Once cool, discard the sachet, and drain the beans and set aside.

In a large Dutch oven over medium-low heat, heat the tomatoes and butter beans with the pork cooking liquid until they start to bubble. Add the garlic butter and stir until completely combined. Fold in the dumplings and pork and cook until heated through and combined, about 4 minutes. Remove from the heat, add the unsalted butter and stir gently until completely melted and incorporated. Season with the lemon juice.

Ladle hefty spoonfuls of the pork and dumplings into bowls and serve with the Parmigiano-Reggiano for sprinkling.

Macaroni au Gratin

Macaroni au Gratin is, of course, a fancy name for mac and cheese. In this case though, it really is so much more than your run-of-the-mill mac. This dish is one of our most beloved offerings, and this year we are on track to sell nearly fifteen thousand orders. Yes, our Macaroni au Gratin has some serious fans. It is unequivocally our most ordered dish.

Coincidentally, it was one of the first dishes I imagined for the menu at Poole's. I knew it had to be there and that we could make it great within the constructs of the Poole's menu ethic: simple classics, pulled apart and reimagined and put back together thoughtfully.

Mac and cheese is, for many, one of those dishes that you just can't resist ordering, regardless of what kind of restaurant you're sitting in. Much like a pile of crispy *pommes frites*, when a Macaroni au Gratin is walked through the dining room at Poole's, heads turn, and the phrase "I'll take one of those" echoes through the joint.

The Poole's Macaroni au Gratin is made to order and is composed of cream (reduced), macaroni elbows (slightly al dente), three cheeses (Jarlsberg, *grana padano*, and sharp white Vermont cheddar), and sea salt. The most important ingredient, though, is a pile of tasting spoons. The cook working the mac station spends all night perfecting the texture and seasoning each order before mounding the same three cheeses on top and moving it to the broiler to be brûléed to a caramelized crisp of bubbling, cheesy perfection (or as close to perfection as we can get).

I can't think of a better representation of my cooking goals than this mac; I hope that, in the attention paid to every detail in such an unassuming dish, the mac communicates that we care about the person who ordered it and about how our food made them feel.

The Macaroni au Gratin is also a bit of a barometer for the growth of our little diner. In the early months, Sunny Gerhart, my first sous chef at Poole's, and I would arrive at the restaurant shortly after daybreak, though it seemed we'd just left a few hours before (because we had). We'd hop on the day's tasks, one of which was always grating the cheeses for the Macaroni au Gratin. At the time, we grated every bit of the cheese on a household box grater. As Poole's found its stride, we hired more cooks, and yes, we finally bought a food processor with a cheese grating attachment. These days, it would be hard to imagine grating the amount of cheese that's required to keep the mac gooey and irresistible (more than ten thousand pounds of cheese per year), but it warms my heart to remember that the box grating task used to get me out of bed before the sun came up.

As I hand off the recipe to our most popular dish at Poole's Diner, I'm not worried about sabotaging our business. Though I'm sure you can justify rolling this recipe out on a holiday or special occasion, I'm well aware of all of the guilt associated with cooking anything at home with this many calories in it. That kind of guilt is what restaurants are for . . . so come on in, you can blame us. **SERVES 4**

Kosher salt

6 ounces dry elbow macaroni (about 1¼ cups)

1 teaspoon neutral vegetable oil

2 ounces grana padano, shredded

2 ounces Jarlsberg, shredded

6 ounces white cheddar, shredded

2 cups heavy cream

Sea salt

In a medium saucepan, bring 2 quarts water and 1½ tablespoons kosher salt to a boil. Add the macaroni and return to a boil; once boiling, cook until barely al dente (about 5 minutes), then drain the pasta well. Transfer to a rimmed baking sheet and mix in the oil to keep the noodles from sticking. Let cool completely. You should have about 3 cups.

Set a rack in the oven about 4 inches from the broiler and preheat the broiler. Combine the *grana padano*, Jarlsberg, and white cheddar in a large bowl; reserve 60 percent of the cheese for the top.

In a large deep saucepan, bring the cream and 1 teaspoon sea salt to a boil. Let simmer for about 2 minutes. The cream will foam up and then subside into a simmer. Add the noodles and cook, stirring occasionally, about 90 seconds. The cream will start to thicken just slightly and coat the noodles. Start adding 40 percent of the cheese in small handfuls, stirring and waiting for each addition to melt and incorporate into the sauce before adding more. Transfer the contents of the pan to a 2½-quart skillet or baking dish, mound the reserved cheese over the top, and place the dish on a baking sheet to catch any drips. Place the baking sheet under the broiler for 3 to 5 minutes, rotating throughout, until the cheese melts and caramelizes into a golden-brown crust.

Watch it carefully, as every broiler is different. Remove the gratin from the oven and let it rest 5 minutes. Serve immediately.

Grits with Roasted Pumpkin, Aged Maple Syrup, and Crispy Pepitas

A bowl of grits is an icon of Southern cuisine and a staple of the region's breakfast menus. Thanks to the work of artisanal millers such as Anson Mills and Geechie Boy, grits have grown from their casual roots into something more refined. This dish continues down that trajectory, injecting the grains with the earthy-sweet flavor of roasted pumpkin and adding the rich sugar of barrel-aged maple syrup. While I'm usually sensitive to sweetness in savory dishes, here it's a tool to amplify the natural sugars of the corn so use the best grits you can get your hands on. **SERVES 4**

1 (1¾-pound) pumpkin

Olive oil

Sea salt

1 cup heavy cream

1 cup stone-ground white corn grits

¼ cup finely grated
    Parmigiano-Reggiano

Juice of ½ lemon

½ cup barrel-aged maple syrup

Preheat a convection oven to 350°F (or a regular oven to 375°F).

Halve the pumpkin vertically. Scrape out the seeds and set aside; rub the interior of the pumpkin with olive oil and dust generously with salt. Place cut side up on a baking sheet and bake for 30 minutes. Flip the halves and bake for 20 minutes more. Let the pumpkin cool slightly. When cool enough to handle, scoop out the flesh, transfer to a food processor, and puree until smooth. Set aside.

Meanwhile, wash the reserved pumpkin seeds well and measure out ½ cup (discard the rest or save for another use). Place the seeds in a bowl and drizzle with 1 teaspoon olive oil and ¼ teaspoon salt. Toss to coat. Place a baking sheet in the oven for 5 minutes to preheat. Add the seeds to the hot pan and bake for 18 to 20 minutes, until crispy and lightly golden.

In a large saucepan, bring 4 cups water, the cream, and 1 teaspoon salt to a boil. Stir in the grits and reduce to a simmer. Cook, stirring occasionally, until the grits are tender and thick, about 50 minutes. Remove from the heat and stir in the pumpkin puree, Parmigiano-Reggiano, and lemon juice.

Divide the grits among bowls, sprinkle the pumpkin seeds over each bowl, and drizzle with the maple syrup.

Short Rib Pot Pie

Pot pie is one of the more signature dishes on menus at most American diners. It delivers the warmth of a rich stew in a flaky pastry package. The filling is negotiable, depending on the time of year and the story of the cook steering the stove. It's a dish that simply exudes comfort, no matter where you come from.

In this version, we make use of our short rib recipe (page 213), pairing it with Charred Onions (page 91) and roasted root vegetables. Though there are many options for encasing the filling in pastry, I prefer the "island" approach. I focus my energy on nailing the textures and flavors of the filling, and I float a crispy pastry layer on top. This approach yields a crunchy, flaky dough that takes a dip into the gravy on your command with the press a spoon. It's a simple technique, even for an entry level pastry cook.

Though the "gravy" in most pot pie is generally fairly thick, you'll find this one lighter in viscosity. With all of these rich flavors, I really like the sauce holding everything together to be a bit delicate.

Float the island technique on your favorite flavor of pot pie, swapping our proteins and vegetables as you see fit, or as the season inspires. **SERVES 8**

CORNMEAL CRUST

1¼ cups all-purpose flour

¼ cup fine-ground cornmeal

1 teaspoon kosher salt

½ cup cold unsalted butter, cut into cubes

Ice water

1 medium (¾-pound) rutabaga

1 medium (¾-pound) sweet potato

3 tablespoons olive oil

2 teaspoons sea salt

3 tablespoons neutral vegetable oil

3 cloves garlic

2 tablespoons unsalted butter

To make the cornmeal crust, in a large bowl whisk together the flour, cornmeal, and salt. Add the ½ cup butter and place in the freezer for 1 hour. Transfer to a food processor and pulse until the butter is in small pea-size pieces. While pulsing, drizzle in the ice water, 1 tablespoon at a time. Add just enough so that the flour, when pinched, sticks together. Turn the dough out onto a work surface and press together into a round. Wrap in plastic and refrigerate for 1 hour (or up to overnight).

Remove the dough from the refrigerator. Lightly flour a work surface, and roll the dough out to ¼ inch thickness. Cut a round of parchment that is 8½ inches in diameter (if using a 9-inch pie dish; otherwise, cut the round ½ inch smaller than the diameter of your baking dish). Use the parchment as a guide, and cut the dough into a circle of the same size. Place the dough on the parchment and transfer to a baking sheet. Score the top of the dough in a cross-hatch pattern, then transfer the baking sheet to the freezer for 1 hour.

1½ pounds cooked short rib meat (see page 213), cut into 1-inch cubes

1 cup diced Charred Onion (page 91)

3 medium thyme sprigs

1 bunch Lacinato kale, tough stems removed, leaves cut into 1-inch pieces

1½ cups Rich Beef Stock (page 25)

2 tablespoons Roasted Garlic Butter (page 20)

Preheat a convection oven to 350°F (or a regular oven to 375°F).

Place the pie crust in the oven and bake for 15 to 20 minutes, rotating every 5 minutes, until golden and crisp around the edges. Set aside while you prepare the filling. Increase the oven temperature to 375°F (400°F in a regular oven).

To make the filling, peel and dice the rutabaga and sweet potato into ½-inch cubes. In a large bowl, toss with the olive oil and salt. Transfer to a parchment lined baking sheet and bake for 10 to 15 minutes, until just tender. Let cool.

In a large, high-sided sauté pan, heat the neutral vegetable oil over medium heat. When it shimmers, add the garlic and cook, stirring, until they are toasted, about 3 minutes. Add 1 tablespoon of the unsalted butter. Once it has melted, add the short rib in a single layer. Cook, undisturbed for 2 minutes to help caramelize. Using a rubber spatula, stir the short ribs, then season lightly with salt. Cook 2 more minutes, stirring, to continue to caramelize the short ribs.

Stir in the onions and thyme. Fold in the kale and cook until it wilts and reduces down, about 2 minutes. The moisture the kale releases will help to deglaze the pan.

Add the Rich Beef Stock and increase the heat to high to bring to a boil. Reduce to a simmer and cook 3 to 4 minutes, until the sauce begins to look viscous. Add the garlic butter and swirl to combine. When it's melted, fold in the reserved roasted root vegetables.

Pour the contents of the pan into a 9½-inch deep dish pie pan or a 2-quart soufflé dish. Place the prebaked crust on top. Melt the remaining tablespoon unsalted butter and brush the top of the crust.

Bake for 10 minutes. Rotate the pan, then cook an additional 5 minutes until the pie is bubbling. Brush the crust with the remaining melted butter and serve immediately.

Meat & Fish

I reject the notion that you need meat or fish at the center of your meal. The prescribed formula for an "entrée"—protein accompanied by a vegetable and a starch—feels formulaic and isn't always how I want to eat. So I've taken to the strategy of treating meat or fish almost like some people treat a side: on its own, stripped of the accessories.

This accomplishes a few things: it allows me to mix and match my meal depending on how I'm feeling. While the roast chicken on page 202 is a happy bedfellow to the mashed potatoes on page 151, I see no issue with piling the thighs on top of a pile of greens from the Vinaigrettes chapter, if that's what I'm craving. You should exercise equal abandon.

Isolating these dishes from their usual counterparts also weakens the mainstream idea that we should be eating meat or fish at every meal. The reality is that our oceans are overfished and meat production requires far more energy than plant production. The least we can do as conscientious eaters is to treat meat and fish as special, rather than as a default source of calories.

Luckily, many of these recipes, while classic in their bones, have elements of celebration in them. Every time I make Poole's Steak (page 217), it feels like I'm treating myself to one of life's small luxuries. And Slow Shrimp with Marinated Peppers (page 229) feels as indulgent as a lobster tail. I hope they feel just as special to you.

Cast-Iron Roast Chicken with Garlic and Herbs

"What would your last meal on earth be?" seems like a somber question, but for a cook, the answer is usually front of mind. If you asked me what my favorite thing to *cook* is, I would fumble for an answer. But this question? Easy. My send off from this joyous place would be simple roast chicken. Without a doubt.

I remember when chicken was considered the bummer dish on a restaurant menu, as in, "Why would you order chicken in a restaurant?" The conventional wisdom was that restaurants served chicken out of necessity to placate picky or timid eaters. It became a totem of boring, bland food. This infuriates me. I've always found chicken so rewarding, and I try to honor it every time I cook it.

My love for simple roast chicken no doubt originates from the roast chicken for two at Zuni Café in San Francisco, a dish loved by many. Though the dish was built for two, not even my occasional visits as a solo diner could deter me from ordering the bird. The servers never seem fazed by this request, which makes me think I was not alone.

Roast chicken is a regular feature on the menu at Poole's, as well as in my home kitchen, where I use a longer, slower roasting period to render the skin extra crispy and the flesh extra tender. **SERVES 4**

Kosher salt

3 tablespoons sugar

1 (3½-pound) whole chicken, quartered, backbones and wingtips removed (reserve these for making stock later)

2 tablespoons neutral vegetable oil

1 head garlic, halved across the equator

2 rosemary sprigs

4 thyme sprigs

2 tablespoons unsalted butter

Juice of ½ lemon

1 tablespoon olive oil

Combine 6 tablespoons salt, the sugar, and 4 cups water in a large pot and stir until the salt and sugar dissolve. Add 4 more cups cold water. Add the chicken pieces. Cover and refrigerate for 8 to 12 hours. Remove the chicken from the brine, discard the brine, and pat the pieces dry.

Place a rack in the bottom third of the oven and preheat a convection oven to 300°F (or a regular oven to 325°F). In a large cast-iron skillet over medium heat, heat the vegetable oil until it shimmers. Season the chicken lightly with salt and place the pieces, skin side down, in the skillet, with as much of the skin in contact with the surface of the pan as possible. Cook for 1 minute, then place the garlic, cut side down, in the pan, along with the rosemary and thyme. Let sear until the herbs and garlic are very aromatic, 4 to 5 minutes, then move the herbs and garlic to the tops of the chicken pieces (so that they don't burn but are still giving off flavor). Continue cooking until the skin is very crisp (lift up a piece of chicken to take a peek), about 3 minutes. Cut the butter into four equal pieces and place one on top of each piece of chicken.

Slide the pan into the oven and cook for 30 minutes. Flip the chicken and increase the oven temperature to 450°F (475°F in a regular oven). Cook for an additional 10 minutes, watching closely to make sure the chicken doesn't brown too quickly. Remove the skillet from the oven and transfer the chicken pieces, skin-side up, to a wire rack. Let rest for a minimum of 10 minutes.

Remove the herbs and garlic from the skillet (you can garnish the chicken with the cloves from the roasted garlic if you like) and pour the drippings into a small saucepan. Once the chicken has rested 10 minutes, bring the contents of the saucepan to a simmer over medium heat; cut the heat and whisk in the lemon juice and olive oil.

Place the chicken on a platter, drizzle with the pan sauce (and garnish with the garlic cloves if you like), and serve.

Buttermilk Fried Chicken with Hot Honey

My mother's fried chicken was one of the more regularly occurring meals in our home. The recipe was one of the many gifts passed down from her grandmother, and mom could execute it with her eyes closed. And from the sounds and smells, I could tell you exactly what step she was on with mine closed too. I'd hear the current-driven ping as she fired up the electric skillet to heat the oil. It sat on an open counter, and I'd smell the change in temperature in the oil. Next, the sound of the chicken splashing in a bowl of buttermilk, followed by the raindrop effect as she lifted it from the bowl and allowed the excess buttermilk to drip away. As she added the pieces to a paper shopping bag filled with seasoned flour, they'd make a sort of dramatic thud. The crinkling sound of the thick brown paper would cue that she was rolling down the top of the bag into her grip; she would then vigorously shake the bag to coat every nook and crease of the chicken. I would hear a Rice Krispie-like crackle as she tested the temperature of the oil with a drip of buttermilk, followed by a shower of bubbling as she lowered the chicken into the liquid. The room would fill with the smell of the crisping batter and, as it cooked, of rich chicken stock. These two smells in combination are purely magical to me. (You can open your eyes now.)

Mom would rest the chicken on paper towel–coated plates. It would hit the table just barely warm. This meant the chicken was crunchy but fully rested at the bone. To heat it in the oven before serving would threaten this near-perfect state, so warm over hot was always a compromise worth making. We always served the chicken with honey harvested from my father's beehives.

I'm sure it's clear by now: I am a fried chicken purist. The recipe from Poole's is a riff on Mom's classic, with the update of brine (neither she nor I had heard of such a thing back then). Though the chicken is straightforward, the spiced honey sets this recipe apart. **SERVES 4**

Continued

Combine 6 tablespoons salt, the sugar, and 4 cups water in a large pot and stir until the salt and sugar dissolve. Add 4 more cups cold water. Add the chicken pieces. Cover and refrigerate for 8 to 12 hours. Remove the chicken from the brine, discard the brine, and pat the chicken pieces dry.

Kosher salt

3 tablespoons sugar

1 whole chicken, cut into 8 pieces

Neutral vegetable oil, for frying

4 cups all-purpose flour

4 cups whole buttermilk

HOT HONEY

½ cup honey

1 clove garlic, crushed

5 small thyme sprigs

1 rosemary sprig

3 dried pequín chiles
   (or chiles de àrbol)

1 tablespoon unsalted butter

When you're ready to fry the chicken, pour enough oil into a large cast-iron skillet to come halfway up the sides and heat until it reaches 325°F on a deep-fry thermometer. Meanwhile, put the flour and 1 teaspoon salt in a paper grocery bag, fold closed, and shake to combine. Fill a large bowl with the buttermilk. Line a baking sheet with paper towels.

Remove the chicken pieces from the brine and pat them dry. Discard the brine. One by one, dip the chicken pieces in the buttermilk, lift to drain the excess back into the bowl, then place in the grocery bag with the flour mixture. When all of the chicken is in the bag, fold the bag closed and shake for about 30 seconds to coat the chicken thoroughly with the flour mixture.

Lift the chicken pieces from the bag and shake off the excess flour. Add the pieces to the skillet, making sure not to crowd the pan and adjusting the heat of the oil as necessary to maintain 325°F. Fry the pieces, turning once, until done (155°F on the interior for white meat, 165°F on the interior for dark meat); this will take about 9 minutes for wings and drumsticks, 11 to 12 minutes for thighs and breasts. Transfer the chicken to the lined baking sheet and let rest for at least 10 minutes.

While the chicken rests, make the hot honey. Warm the honey, garlic, thyme, rosemary, and chiles in a small saucepan over low heat for 5 minutes; the honey will begin to foam slightly. Remove from the heat and add the butter, gently swirling until it's completely melted.

Arrange the chicken on a platter and spoon some of the hot honey and herbs over the top of the chicken. Pass around the remaining honey on the side.

The thigh is my favorite part of the chicken; it's rich, meaty, and full of flavor. I'll always unapologetically take the last thigh as the platter is passed around the dinner table.

At Poole's, we sell a lot of what's referred to as the airline cut—a breast with the wing drumette attached—which leaves us with a pile of delicious dark meat (a great problem to have, in my opinion. This recipe banks on it. It is a riff on one of my favorite dishes, *saltimbocca* (Italian for "jumps in the mouth"). Though saltimbocca is classically made with veal, the chicken thighs pair perfectly with the salty ham and fresh sage, and this fresh take on tomato gravy adds a little more of the *jump* that earned this classic its name. **SERVES 4**

ROSEMARY TOMATO GRAVY

2½ pounds Roma tomatoes

2 teaspoons sea salt

½ cup olive oil

4 cloves garlic, smashed

4 (3-inch) rosemary sprigs

2 tablespoons unsalted butter

2 pounds boneless, skinless chicken thighs

4 large fresh sage leaves, finely minced

4 tablespoons Dijon mustard

3 ounces thinly sliced prosciutto

1 cup all-purpose flour

4 large eggs, beaten

3 cups panko

Sea salt

½ cup olive oil

Continued

To make the gravy, slice the stem end off of each Roma tomato, then grate the tomatoes on the large holes of a box grater, discarding the skins. Season with the sea salt and set aside.

In a large deep skillet over medium heat, warm the olive oil until it shimmers. Add the garlic and cook, stirring frequently, until the garlic is fragrant and toasted, about 3 minutes. Add the rosemary and cook for 1 minute to toast. Stir in the grated tomatoes and bring to a simmer; cook for 5 minutes. Reduce the heat and keep the mixture warm while you prepare the chicken.

Divide the chicken evenly among four resealable quart-size plastic freezer bags. Do not seal. Use a meat mallet to pound out the chicken to a ¼-inch-thick square that fills the bag. Place the bags in the freezer and chill for 15 minutes. Meanwhile, in a small bowl, mix together the sage and Dijon.

Pull one chicken bag from the freezer, remove the meat from the bag, and place it on a work surface. Rub both sides with a quarter of the mustard mixture, then lay 2 prosciutto slices on one half of the chicken layer. Fold the other half of the chicken over the prosciutto, sandwiching it. Transfer the chicken cutlet to a small baking sheet and return it to the freezer. Repeat with the remaining three chicken portions, working one at a time, and keeping the others in the freezer while you work.

Preheat a convection oven to 350°F (or a regular oven to 375°F). Put the flour, eggs, and panko in three separate shallow bowls (pie tins work great). Season the flour with 1 teaspoon salt, and season the egg mixture with 1 teaspoon salt. Set a baking sheet next to the workstation. One at a time, dip each chicken cutlet in the flour, then coat in the egg, and then finally coat in the bread crumbs. Place the cutlets on the baking sheet, and top each with a sprinkle of additional breadcrumbs to soak up any wet spots.

In a large skillet, heat the olive oil over medium-high heat. Set a wire rack over a baking sheet and place it next to the stove. Working in batches, add the cutlets to the pan two at a time, and cook undisturbed for 3 minutes, then flip and cook on the other side until golden, an additional 3 minutes. Transfer the cutlets to the prepared rack. When you've fried all four cutlets, transfer to the oven and cook for 8 minutes, or until cooked through. Let the chicken rest for 10 minutes.

To serve, return the tomato gravy to high heat for about 2 minutes to reheat. Remove from the heat and add the butter; swirl the pan until the butter has melted completely. Slice the chicken cutlets into 1-inch-thick slices. Pour a healthy ladle of gravy on a platter, and top with the chicken.

Royale with Cheese

The Royale (the name is a reference to the film *Pulp Fiction*) shouts out to the roadside dive patty melt that also embraces the bistro steak. It's a ten-ounce baseball of meat, ground from the chuck muscle of grass-fed, sustainably raised beef. If you don't have one of those nifty KitchenAid meat grinding attachments for your mixer, this is as good a recipe as any to convince you to buy one. You can also use good-quality ground beef if you're not up for grinding your own.

The beef is rolled in ground toasted Tellicherry pepper and seared in rendered duck fat (putting the royal in Royale). Then we roast it to temperature and top it with a cheese plate–worthy cheese—this is open to your interpretation, but you want a cheese that will melt well; we've topped the Royale with everything from an artisanal smoked cheddar to a creamy local blue cheese. I like my Royale medium-rare and topped with Carr Valley Mobay (a domestic version of Morbier). We serve it open-faced over grilled brioche, with a side of red wine–shallot jus. It's a knife-and-fork experience. When pals are visiting the restaurant, we'll take the liberty of parting the center of their Royale with two back-to-back sporks and pouring the jus directly into the center. It travels through the patty and into the brioche, creating one of the most delectable savory bread puddings imaginable.

When we opened our burger joint, Chuck's, we moved the Royale off of the every-day Poole's menu and gave it its own day: Royale Sunday. I still remember a guest coming in on a Friday and being extremely disgruntled by this news. He sent a message to me through his server: "Tell her she's crazy . . . this place will never make it without the Royale. You'll be closed in six months." It's good to have enthusiasts (even when they're a little crazy). Well Mr. Angry Guy, four years later we're still here, and Royale Sunday continues to bring friends and strangers together for one of our favorite plates. **SERVES 4**

Continued

To make the jus, in a 2-quart saucepan over medium heat, heat the oil. When it shimmers, place the garlic in the pan, cut side down, then add the shallots. Cook, stirring occasionally, for 5 minutes, until they start to caramelize. Increase the heat to high for 3 minutes, stirring frequently. Add the peppercorn, bay, and thyme. Toast, stirring for 2 minutes.

BEEF-SHALLOT JUS

2 tablespoons neutral vegetable oil

2 heads garlic, halved across
   the equator

6 shallots, quartered

1 teaspoon black peppercorn

1 medium fresh bay leaf, torn

4 medium thyme sprigs

1 (750-ml) bottle red wine

1 tablespoon honey

4 cups Rich Beef Stock
   (page 25)

Sea salt

2½ pounds beef chuck with fat-
   cap intact (or high-quality
   85 percent lean ground beef)

½ cup finely ground toasted
   Tellicherry pepper, sifted

½ cup rendered duck fat

4 ounces meltable, cheese
   plate–worthy cheese

1 tablespoon neutral vegetable oil

1 tablespoon unsalted butter

4 (½-inch-thick) slices brioche

Remove from heat and add the wine. Return to high heat. Add the honey and bring to a simmer; reduce the mixture for 20 minutes, or until the bubbles in the liquid reveal the bottom of the pan (it will be thick and syrupy). Add the beef stock and return to a boil. Reduce the heat to medium and simmer the sauce for 18 to 20 minutes, or until reduced by half. Strain the sauce and discard the solids (you should have about 2 cups). Season the sauce with sea salt to taste. The sauce can be made up to 6 days in advance and refrigerated in a lidded container.

To make the Royales, dice the chuck into 1-inch cubes and place in the freezer for 15 minutes to chill. Run the cubes through a meat grinder using the coarsest die. Run the ground meat through the grinder a second time, then portion it into four 10-ounce balls. Throw each ball back and forth between your hands with a good amount of force, like you're warming up your arm to throw the first pitch. Do this for 1 to 2 minutes; the meat will become slightly creamier as the proteins in the meat break down and emulsify with the fats. (It's important to do this for a full minute at least; it makes a huge difference in the texture of the patty when cooked.)

Heat a cast-iron skillet over high heat. Preheat a convection oven to 450°F (or a regular oven to 475°F). Season the patties all over with a generous dusting of sea salt. Pour the pepper onto a flat work surface and roll each patty in the pepper so it's completely coated. Add half of the duck fat to the hot skillet. When the duck fat is melted and shimmering, add 2 patties to the skillet. Sear the patties on one side until they form a nice crust, about 2 minutes, then flip and sear on the other side, 1 to 2 minutes more. Transfer to a baking sheet. Carefully wipe out the skillet, return to high heat, and repeat with the remaining duck fat and patties.

Return the first 2 patties to the skillet and transfer all 4 patties to the oven. Cook for 5 minutes for medium-rare; remove from the oven and divide the cheese among the patties, then return to the oven and cook for another 90 seconds, just until the cheese melts. Transfer the Royales to a cooling rack and let rest while you toast the brioche.

In a large skillet over high heat, heat the oil. When it shimmers, add the butter and place the pieces of brioche in the skillet. Toast for 2 minutes until golden brown on one side.

Place a piece of brioche, toasted side up, on each plate and top with a patty. Serve with a small pitcher of jus for dressing at the table.

Short Ribs, the Simplest Way

After years of making short ribs in all kinds of ways, from searing and braising on the stove to grilling over high heat, we came up with this dead-simple method and have never looked back. It truly is the simplest way and produces delicious, thoroughly seasoned ribs that are endlessly versatile. Throw the meat into a potpie (see page 196), toss it with dumplings, serve it over potato salad, glaze it with pepper jelly: this recipe is just the beginning. **SERVES 6**

5 pounds bone-in beef
    short rib slab

Sea salt

Black pepper in a mill

2 cups red wine

1 head garlic, halved
    across the equator

8 thyme sprigs

4 rosemary sprigs

Preheat a convection oven to 450°F (or a regular oven to 475°F).

Dust the short ribs on all sides with salt and pepper so they are well coated. Place the ribs in a large roasting pan and roast for 20 minutes, or until they have a nice caramelized crust. Remove from the oven and reduce the oven to 250°F convection (275°F regular).

Let the ribs rest for 10 minutes, then add the wine and 2 cups water to the bottom of the pan. Place the garlic halves, thyme, and rosemary in the pan as well. Cover the pan tightly with foil and return to the oven. Roast for 4 hours, until the short ribs are very tender but not falling apart. Remove from the oven and turn up the corners of the foil, while still keeping the pan mostly covered (this will release the residual heat gradually so the short ribs retain most of their juices). Let rest for 20 minutes. To serve, slice the ribs between the bones and divide among plates, or alternatively, cut the entire slab off the bone and cut into 1-inch-thick slices.

note: If you're making the ribs to use the meat in the Short Rib Pot Pie (page 196) or the Short Rib Hash (page 215), let the meat cool completely, then cut from the bone and dice into ¾-inch cubes. Refrigerate until ready to use.

When we first opened Poole's, we served brunch. From the gate, it was one of our most popular services. The line would begin to form around 10:30, and by the time we opened, there were enough people waiting that the entire restaurant would immediately fill up.

A few years later, when we were opening our coffee shop, Joule, we decided that the Poole's brunch menu would have a better home there. So Poole's became a dinner-only restaurant, but not without some sadness. The last brunch shift at Poole's was packed with regulars, coming to have one last cup of coffee and share in the magic of something that was growing up.

At one of those last Poole's brunches, one of our guests, Robbie, after finishing his meal, asked the hostess for a piece of paper. Supplied with Post-Its, he proceeded to write a poem and asked that it be delivered to me.

I've saved the note to this day because it's a beautiful reminder that restaurants are shared spaces. The best restaurant experiences give us a sense of ownership. They provide us with a comfort that we can rely on and feel a part of. That feeling is the truest definition of hospitality.

Every single person who walks into Poole's has contributed to what it is, what it is becoming. And for all of the eggs and biscuits and gravy that made up the Poole's brunch, it was really about that shared energy, that special communion, that ritual of gathering with a bunch of people to linger over coffee. So in honor of those many shared Sundays, here's the recipe that Robbie requested. **SERVES 6 to 8**

Short Rib Hash

How I long for days gone past
When Poole's served their short rib hash
Potatoes, eggs and mustard gravy
and slow cooked beef, oh baby!

Why would this dish just disappear?
I think now its been almost a year
All these ingredients are in the kitchen
But togetherness is what we're missin'

I've begun to worry about the fate
of this continued missing plate
Like challah has.it bee n your lasthour?
Were you also traded for something sour?

So to the menu planner I plea
bring back the hash just for me!

— Robbie Taylor

P.S. I'd also like to take this time to suggest naming a sandwich "The Robbie" at the Wilmoore Redo.

1 cup milk

1 cup heavy cream

1 tablespoon unsalted butter

2 tablespoons all-purpose flour

1 tablespoon whole-grain mustard

2 teaspoons Dijon mustard

½ cup grated Parmigiano-Reggiano

Sea salt

Black pepper in a mill

SHORT RIB HASH

Neutral vegetable oil

1 medium yellow onion (about
    8 ounces), julienned

Sea salt

2 pounds Yukon gold potatoes

Kosher salt

4 tablespoons unsalted butter,
    melted

Black pepper in a mill

1 pound cold cooked short rib meat,
    diced (see page 213)

Poached eggs, to serve (optional)

First, make the gravy. Combine the milk and cream in a saucepan over medium heat and bring to a simmer. Turn the heat down to low.

In a separate saucepan, melt the butter over low heat. Add the flour and whisk until smooth. Continue to stir for 3 to 4 minutes. Add the hot cream mixture and stir until fully incorporated. Increase the heat to medium and bring to a simmer, then return to low heat and stir for 5 to 6 minutes. Taste to confirm that the flour is fully cooked into the cream mixture (you shouldn't be able to taste the grain of the flour). Stir in the mustards and the cheese. Season to taste with salt and pepper and keep warm.

To make the hash, in a skillet over medium heat, heat 1 tablespoon oil until it shimmers. Add the onions and season generously with sea salt. Stir the onions to coat and cook until tender and slightly caramelized, about 12 minutes. Transfer from the pan to a large mixing bowl and set aside.

Quarter the potatoes lengthwise and slice into ½-inch-thick pieces. Place in a pot with 3 quarts water and ¼ cup kosher salt. Bring to a boil over high heat and immediately reduce to a simmer. Let cook until slightly tender but not falling apart, 5 to 6 minutes. Drain and place in one layer on a baking sheet to cool. Let cool for 5 minutes and then add the potatoes to the bowl with the onions. Add the butter, 2 teaspoons sea salt, and 15 cranks of the pepper mill. Mix to coat the potatoes and onions evenly.

In a 12-inch cast-iron skillet over medium-high heat, heat 2 table-spoons oil until shimmering. Add the diced short ribs to the pan, season the meat with 1 teaspoon sea salt, and, using a spatula, flip the rib pieces to sear all sides. Add the potato and onion mixture to the pan and press in a flat layer over the meat. Reduce the heat to medium.

Let the contents of the pan crisp on the bottom side for about 3 minutes. Then use the spatula to flip the hash, one spatula scoop at a time, until the seared side is facing up. Repeat this process multiple times, letting each side sear for 3 minutes, or until the majority of the hash is caramelized and crisp. I spend about 15 minutes on this task, and it yields a beautifully caramelized and flavorful hash. If you like more crispy bits in your hash, continue the process until you are satisfied.

Serve the hash with the mustard gravy ladled over the top and with poached eggs, if you like.

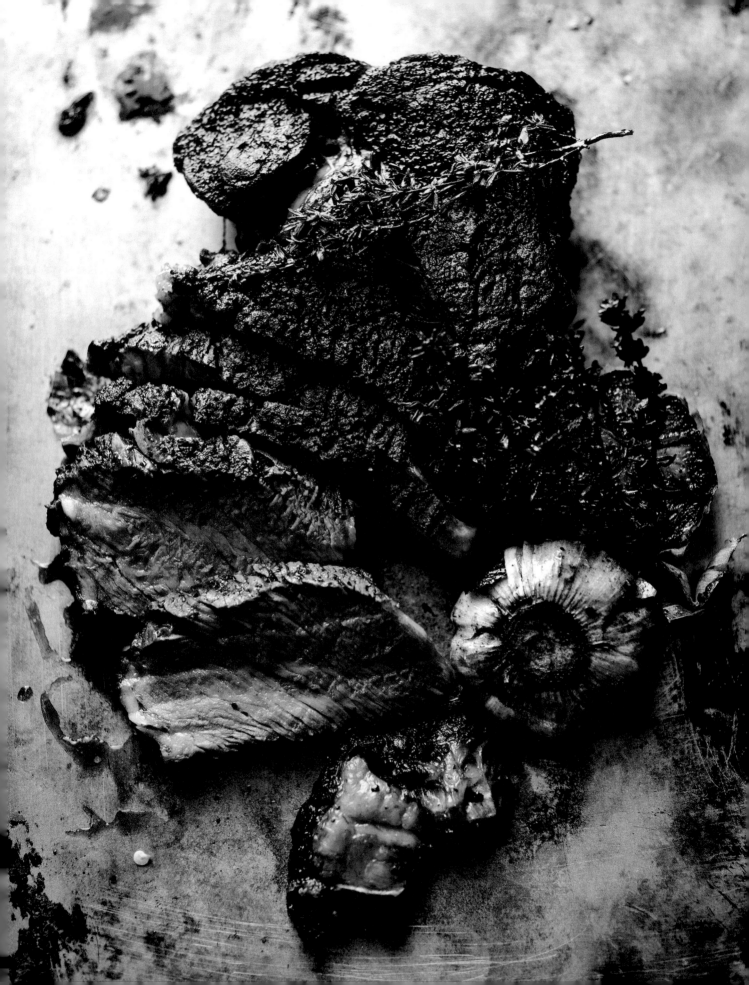

Poole's Steak

Steak is a unicorn dish for us, one that we serve only as a special, only when the mood strikes us, and only as a big cut, usually served for two. Every time we feature it, it sells out halfway through dinner service.

So why this sporadic attitude toward a dish that so many of our guests seem to love? Because, to me, steak is a special-occasion meal, something that can turn a regular old Tuesday night into an event. I think that's even more the case when you're not planning for it. An unexpected steak dinner for two is the type of experience that sums up pretty accurately the way that I think about what we try to create with Poole's Diner. It has enough casual flexibility to happen anytime, but it leaves you feeling like you experienced something special.

Pair this steak with a glass of chilled Beaujolais, a plate of the herb-scented mashed potatoes on page 151, and a giant pile of Bibb Lettuce Salad (page 87). **SERVES 2**

1 big (36- to 42-ounce) steak, 1½ inches thick, bone in (rib eye, porterhouse, or strip would all work well here)

Sea salt

Black pepper in a mill

2 tablespoons neutral vegetable oil

1 head garlic, halved across the equator

4 thyme sprigs

3 tablespoons cold unsalted butter, cut into cubes

½ cup red table wine

Continued

Preheat a convection oven to 450°F (or a regular oven to 475°F).

Let the steak sit at room temperature for 1 hour. Generously season both sides of the steak with salt and then with several cranks of the pepper mill.

Heat the oil in a large cast-iron skillet over medium-high heat. Once the oil begins to shimmer, carefully place the steak in the pan. Place the garlic halves face down in the pan around the steak, along with the sprigs of thyme. Allow the steak to sear and caramelize and the garlic and thyme to become aromatic, about 4 minutes. Add 1 tablespoon of the butter to the pan and swirl to melt. The milk solids in the butter will slow the cooking of the garlic and herbs and release the steak's seared surface from the pan.

Using tongs or a fork, flip the steak. Transfer the garlic and thyme to the top of the steak (the seared side) and add the second tablespoon of butter to the pan. Using a dry towel to hold the handle, tilt the skillet toward you. Use a spoon to gather the melted herb-and-garlic-scented brown butter and baste the steak with it. Continue this process for 2 minutes, then transfer the skillet to the oven.

Allow the steak to roast in the oven until it reaches your desired temperature. I dig my steak medium-rare, which, depending on the size of the steak, could take from 8 to 12 minutes in the oven. Allow the steak to rest for 10 minutes before slicing or serving.

While the steak is resting, transfer the drippings from the cast-iron skillet, including the garlic and herbs, to a stainless-steel pan. Place over high heat and, once the contents of the pan begins to sizzle, deglaze with the wine. Allow the wine to reduce by half and then stir in the remaining 1 tablespoon butter. Season to taste with salt.

Serve the red wine pan sauce over the steak.

Rabbit Poblanos Rellenos with Charred Chile Sauce

Years ago, when I was the chef at a restaurant called Enoteca Vin, one of the dishwashers blew my mind with his technique for chiles rellenos. Up until that point, the only chiles rellenos I'd had were dredged in flour and deep-fried. Ruben was coating the stuffed peppers in a pillowy coating of egg whites and searing them carefully in a pan. This technique produced a light-as-air, almost crepe-like crust that seemed to barely clasp the chile.

I was hooked and started thinking about this form of chiles rellenos as the perfect vehicle for a myriad of rich fillings, from shrimp mousse and smoked chicken to roasted winter squash or even sweet potato and goat cheese. Feel free, if rabbit isn't your thing, to swap out for a filling of your choosing. **SERVES 4**

CHARRED CHILE SAUCE

4 Roma tomatoes

1 poblano chile, stemmed and cut into quarters

½ jalapeño chile, stemmed, seeded if you'd like less heat

½ yellow onion

2 cloves garlic

1 teaspoon sea salt

4 medium poblano chiles

1 cup rabbit confit (see page 38)

2 cups all-purpose flour

Sea salt

6 large egg whites

¼ cup neutral vegetable oil

Fresh cilantro leaves, for garnish

Green onions, sliced on the diagonal, for garnish

Lime wedges, for garnish

Countertop Crème Fraîche (page 159) or sour cream, for garnish

Continued

To make the sauce, slice the tomatoes in half across the equator. Using a paper towel, wipe a thin layer of oil over the surface of a cast-iron skillet and set it over high heat. When the skillet is hot, add the tomato halves, cut side down, along with the poblano, jalapeño, onion, and garlic. Cook until the vegetables are charred on one side, about 4 minutes, then flip and cook for another 2 minutes to cook the peppers all the way through. Transfer the vegetables to a small saucepan and add water until the vegetables are just barely covered.

Bring to a boil, then reduce to a simmer over low heat. Cook, simmering, for 45 minutes to 1 hour, adding additional water to the pan if the vegetables begin to stick to the bottom. Transfer the ingredients to a blender and puree with the salt until the mixture is a smooth, pourable sauce (add more water if it's too thick). Keep warm while you work on the chiles.

To roast the peppers, place them directly over a high gas flame. Using metal tongs to safely rotate the peppers, char the entire surface of each pepper. My final step in this process is to balance the pepper on its curvy stem end on the grate of the burner to char that part. This ensures the best yield. (If you don't have a gas range, roast the peppers under an oven broiler set on high; rotate them with metal tongs so they char evenly.) Transfer the peppers to a metal bowl and cover tightly with plastic wrap. Let sit for 15 minutes.

Carefully peel the skins off the peppers by rubbing with a paper towel. Make an incision lengthwise along the side of each pepper and use a small spoon to remove the seeds; take care to keep the chile intact.

Using a small spoon or your hands, stuff each chile with rabbit confit so that it is full but not overstuffed, about ¼ cup each. Pull the edges of the incision together so that one overlaps the other. Set the chiles aside.

Place the flour and 1½ teaspoons salt in a shallow bowl. In a large bowl, beat the egg whites with a mixer on high speed until stiff peaks form. Add 1 teaspoon of the flour mixture to the egg whites and whisk to combine. Place a medium skillet over medium heat and add the oil. Preheat a convection oven to 350°F (or a regular oven to 375°F).

Working in batches, place each chile in the flour and turn to completely coat. Then transfer the chile to the bowl with the egg whites and use your hands to coat the chile with a thick coating of egg white. It's not going adhere very gracefully; do what you can to keep the chile well coated as you transfer it to the skillet. Fry until golden brown on the first side, about 4 minutes, then carefully nudge the chile onto its second side and cook an additional 4 minutes. The egg whites will compress quite a bit into a thin, almost crepe-like golden crust. Turn the chile onto its final side and cook for 4 more minutes, or until the crust is golden and cooked evenly. Transfer the chile to a wire rack set over a baking sheet and repeat with the remaining chiles. When all of the chiles have been fried, transfer the baking sheet to the oven and bake for 12 to 15 minutes.

Divide the chiles among four plates and douse each with a generous ladle of the charred chile sauce. Serve with cilantro, green onions, lime wedges, and crème fraîche on the side.

Crispy Flounder

Every trip I've ever made to the coast has always included one meal of simple fried fish—more specifically, flaky white fish caught in the very waters that soak the shore. I've developed a method for seeking out the best purveyors whenever I'm at a new beach. First, stay away from the big, flashy seafood buffets. Instead, hunt down the fish-fry shack that is invariably the local real deal. Look for the place that appears a tad structurally questionable. Picnic-table seating is usually a good sign.

I've seen fish battered all sorts of ways (cornmeal, beer batter, flour-egg-crumb—you name it), but my favorite is a one-two punch of buttermilk and flour, followed by an immediate trip to the fryer. It's super simple, but man oh man does it let the fish sing. Flounder is my favorite catch for frying. I like to serve it with malt mayo spiked with roasted tomatoes and a chopped-up spoonful of the pickled ramps we put up in the spring. But my year-round condiment is bright, barely spicy Chow-Chow (page 224), a Southern relish of shredded cabbage. **SERVES 4**

Neutral vegetable oil, for frying

4 cups all-purpose flour

Sea salt

1 tablespoon freshly ground black pepper

4 cups buttermilk

4 to 6 (6-ounce) flounder fillets

Chow-Chow (page 224)

Basic Malt Mayo (page 21)

In a large, heavy-bottomed pot, heat 4 inches of oil over high heat until it registers 350°F on a deep-fry thermometer.

Place the flour in a shallow mixing bowl. Whisk in 2 tablespoons salt and the pepper. Place the buttermilk in a second mixing bowl and arrange both bowls within easy reach of the stove. Line a baking sheet with paper towels and set near the stove.

Submerge the fillets in the buttermilk to coat. Pull the fillets from the buttermilk, letting any excess liquid drip back into the bowl. Transfer the fillets to the flour mixture and toss to coat completely. Gently lower the coated fillets into the oil and fry for 4 to 5 minutes, until the fish is cooked through. Transfer to the paper towel–lined baking sheet and season with salt.

Serve the fillets with the Chow-Chow and the mayo on the side.

Chow-Chow

Relish, which is technically what this chow-chow is, can iron a very rich recipe into balance. Anything fried can usually benefit from a relish, such as the Crispy Flounder on page 222. But don't stop there. Stewed peas? Delicious with a spoonful of vinegary Chow-Chow. And of course, it'll upgrade any ballpark hot dog. **MAKES four 8-ounce jars**

2 pounds green cabbage, chopped

1¼ pounds red bell peppers, cored, seeded, and finely diced

1¼ pounds yellow bell peppers, cored, seeded, and finely diced

1 small yellow onion, finely diced

4 teaspoons sea salt

BRINE

1½ cups cider vinegar

½ cup sugar

1½ teaspoons ground turmeric

1½ teaspoons celery seed

1½ teaspoons cayenne pepper

1½ teaspoons sea salt

In a medium mixing bowl, combine the cabbage, peppers, and onion. Sprinkle with the salt and mix well. Store in a covered container in the refrigerator overnight to pull out the water from the vegetables. Drain in a colander set in the sink and return the vegetables to the same container. Set aside.

To make the brine, in a medium saucepot, combine the vinegar, sugar, turmeric, celery seed, cayenne, salt, and ½ cup water. Bring to a boil, then remove from the heat.

Pour the hot brine over the vegetables, stirring to coat everything. Allow to cool to room temperature, then divide among four 8-ounce canning jars. Cover and store in the refrigerator for up to 1 month. (This relish can also be processed in a hot water bath and kept at room temperature.)

Cornbread Crab Cakes

Too often, crab cakes are more "cake" than "crab." Crab is expensive, so stretching it out with a heavy addition of bread crumbs is understandable. But when we serve crab cakes at Poole's, we go heavy on the crab, treating them like an entrée to fully showcase their specialness. Crumbled cornbread helps to bind the ingredients, and I like the nutty note that it adds to the sweet, rich crab, but it's just a support: crab is the star of this show.

This dish aches for delicious slaw or salad to go with it. In the fall and winter months, pile the cakes on top of an apple slaw or celery root rémoulade; in the summer, Charred Summer Squash with Fresh Herbs (page 138) would be delicious. In a pinch, a bed of greens dressed in vinaigrette will do the trick. **SERVES 4**

1 pound jumbo lump crabmeat, carefully checked for shell fragments

5 tablespoons cornbread crumbs (see page 100)

3 tablespoons diced celery

¼ cup diced yellow onion

½ teaspoon sea salt

½ teaspoon freshly ground black pepper

2 teaspoons Dijon mustard

1 large egg

1 tablespoon neutral vegetable oil

In a large bowl, combine the crabmeat, cornbread crumbs, celery, onion, salt, pepper, mustard, and egg and mix well. Divide the crab batter into eight equal balls. Form the balls into puck-shaped patties, and place on a baking sheet. Refrigerate for 30 minutes.

Preheat a convection oven to 350°F (or a regular oven to 375°F).

In a large ovenproof skillet, heat the oil over medium-high heat until it shimmers. Add the crab cakes and sear until golden brown, 3 to 4 minutes. Flip and sear on the other side for 1 minute, or until golden brown. Transfer the skillet to the oven for an additional 5 minutes to cook all the way through. Serve hot.

Pan-Roasted Scallops with Olive Gremolata

Need to make an impression in a hurry? Scallops have you covered. This sweet, buttery shellfish cooks in practically no time but has plenty of richness. The oil-cured olive *gremolata* adds bite and the requisite bitterness to make the sweetness of the scallops truly stand out. We dredge the scallops on one side with Wondra because it creates a paper thin crust that crisps up into a beautiful sear without having to over-cook the scallop itself. Serve these over a bed of the Beluga Lentils with Melted Leeks on page 127. **SERVES 4**

GREMOLATA

¼ cup coarsely chopped
 fresh parsley

½ teaspoon minced garlic

½ teaspoon minced lemon zest

1 tablespoon minced fresh chives

2 tablespoons minced
 oil-cured olives

2 tablespoons neutral vegetable oil

12 U10-size sea scallops
 (about 1½ pounds)

Sea salt

¼ cup Wondra flour

1 tablespoon unsalted butter

To make the *gremolata*, in a small bowl, combine the parsley, garlic, lemon zest, chives, and olives. Mix well, and set aside.

Line a plate with paper towels. Set a large skillet over medium heat and add the oil. Season the scallops on both sides with salt. Place the flour in a shallow dish, and when the oil is shimmering, dip one flat side of each scallop into the flour, shake away any excess, and place the scallop, flour side down, in the skillet. Cook until the edges of the scallop touching the pan are turning a beautiful golden brown and look almost pleated, about 2 minutes. Add the butter to the pan and tilt to swirl it around evenly. Cook for 1 minute more, then flip the scallops.

Tilt the pan toward you and, using a spoon, carefully baste the scallops with the brown butter continually for 2 minutes. Transfer the scallops to the paper towel–lined plate. To serve, place 3 scallops, darkly seared side up, on each plate and garnish with a spoonful of *gremolata*.

Slow Shrimp with Marinated Peppers

I take issue with almost every shrimp scampi dish I've ever had. I love the flavor and the ease with which it comes together, but the shrimp are typically cooked to a texture that can only be described as rubbery.

Shrimp, like any protein, seize and contract when exposed to high heat. I developed this recipe after thinking about ways to avoid that initial high-heat shock to the shrimp, in hope that it would solve my scampi-texture dilemma. My plan worked! Adding the shrimp and butter to a cold pan and heating them slowly together means the shrimp retain a perfectly tender texture and the butter emulsifies into a beautiful silky sauce. **SERVES 4**

½ cup kosher salt

2 cups ice

1½ pounds shrimp (26/30), peeled, deveined, and tails removed

4 tablespoons cold unsalted butter, cut into cubes

1 tablespoon extra-virgin olive oil

½ to ¾ cup drained Marinated Peppers (page 230)

Juice of ½ lemon

Black pepper in a mill

Mix the salt and 4 cups water in a large bowl, stirring until the salt dissolves. Add the ice and the shrimp and let sit for 15 minutes. Drain the shrimp and pat dry.

Place the shrimp in a dry pan with the butter and olive oil. Place the pan over medium heat and start stirring, slowly rolling the shrimp and butter around the pan. Keep stirring constantly; you want to fold the shrimp over in the butter in a slow, continuous motion. The shrimp will cook at around the same speed as the butter melts. Cook until the shrimp are pink throughout and the butter has completely melted into a thick, rich sauce, 7 to 9 minutes. Fold in the peppers and cook for a minute, or until warmed through. Stir in the lemon juice and 2 cranks of the pepper mill. Serve.

Marinated Peppers

This awesome condiment is endlessly versatile, and works beautifully on carpaccio, cooked shrimp, creamy rice grits . . . you name it. The peppers add a tiny piquant punch to nearly any dish you can imagine. They get better with time, so start them the day before you plan to serve them to let the flavors meld. This recipe makes about 1 cup plus oil, which is a bit more than you'll usually need for one meal, but you'll be happy to have some extra lying around. Promise.

MAKES 1 cup

3 large red bell peppers
(about 1½ pounds total)

Sea salt

1 cup olive oil

1 fresh bay leaf

12 thyme sprigs

3 cloves garlic

Zest of 1 lemon, cut into wide
strips with a Y-peeler

To roast the peppers, place them directly over a high gas flame. Using metal tongs to safely rotate the peppers, char the entire surface of each pepper. My final step in this process is to balance the pepper on its curvy stem end on the grate of the burner to char that part. This ensures the best yield. (If you don't have a gas range, roast the peppers under an oven broiler set on high, rotating them with metal tongs so they char evenly.)

Transfer the peppers to a metal bowl and cover with plastic wrap. Let sit for 15 minutes. Use a dish towel to gently rub off the skins of the peppers; don't run them under water, as this will wash away some of the flavor. Tear the peppers in half and remove the stems and seeds. Lay the peppers flat and cut in half horizontally. Slice each half vertically into ¼-inch-wide pieces so that you have batons measuring roughly 2 inches by ¼ inch. Place in a medium bowl and season with ½ teaspoon salt, tossing to distribute.

In a small saucepan, combine the oil, bay, thyme, garlic, and lemon zest. Set over medium heat until the oil begins to slowly bubble. Once it begins bubbling, reduce the heat to low and cook for 4 to 5 minutes more, then remove from the heat. Pour the oil and aromatics over the peppers and let marinate in the refrigerator for at least 6 hours (preferably a day) before using. Pick out and discard the thyme, garlic, bay, and lemon zest before using. The peppers will keep, submerged in their oil in a lidded container in the refrigerator, for up to 2 weeks.

Lamb Meatloaf with Mushroom Pan Gravy

I've always considered meatloaf to be the "blue plate" cousin of the classic meatball. It's essentially an introduction (and fast track) to charcuterie, a terrine in disguise, bound by egg and bread crumb.

I grew up, like so many, on the ground beef version, traditionally capped with a thick and tangy tomato paste slurry. I loved it even as a kid, and I distinctly remember positioning bites of it onto my fork and dragging them (in a snowplow-like pattern) through plumes of mashed potatoes, as the two ingredients made a gravy of their own. My favorite part of the whole ceremony was the next day, when I watched my dad produce his favorite arrangement of leftovers: an ice-cold one-inch slab of the meatloaf, a smear of mayo, two leaves of iceberg lettuce, all rested between two slices of grocery-store rye. His eyebrows would rise in accomplishment as he wrapped his signature sandwich in a paper towel and carried it to his favorite armchair, cold can of beer in hand.

At the time, I was grossed out by the cold slabs of congealed meatloaf. But now, as a cook who considers what it means for food, especially meat, to rest, I realize that my dad was accessing the finest version of the previous night's dinner—rested and holding on to all of the wonderful rich juices that had traveled through the loaf.

Our version at Poole's takes full advantage of this idea, resting the meatloaf fully, and then searing slices individually to create a crispy exterior that contrasts with the succulent center. This recipe allows (actually demands) you to do the heavy lifting in advance and to take advantage of all of the juices heading home to where they belong.

SERVES 8

MEATLOAF

2 pounds ground lamb

1 pound ground pork

3 cloves garlic, pounded into a paste with kosher salt

2 tablespoons Dijon mustard

1 tablespoon sea salt

½ teaspoon ground toasted black pepper

To make the meatloaf, combine the ground lamb and pork, garlic, mustard, sea salt, pepper, fennel seed, panko, onion, and oil in the bowl of a stand mixer fitted with a paddle attachment. Mix on low speed for 4 to 6 minutes. Chill the mixture in the refrigerator for 1 hour.

Preheat a convection oven to 250°F (or a regular oven to 275°F). Grease a 9-by-5-inch loaf pan. Cut a length of parchment paper long enough to line the long sides and bottom of the pan with an inch hanging over the top of the pan's long sides (these will act as handles later to help you ease the loaf out of the pan).

1 teaspoon ground fennel seed

1 cup panko

½ yellow onion, grated on the small holes of a box grater

1 tablespoon neutral vegetable oil

MUSHROOM PAN GRAVY

Neutral vegetable oil

1 pound mushrooms (oysters, chanterelles, or morels all work well), cleaned and cut into bite-size pieces

1 shallot, minced

Sea salt

2 thyme sprigs

½ cup dry white wine

1½ cups Rich Beef Stock (page 25)

½ cup Porcini Butter (page 20), cut into cubes

Use your hands to form the mixture into an oval and place in the prepared loaf pan. Bake for 30 minutes, rotate the pan 180 degrees. Bake for another 40 minutes or until a thermometer inserted into the center of the loaf registers 120°F (the meatloaf will continue to cook while it rests). Remove from the oven and let the loaf rest for at least 30 minutes.

Meanwhile, make the mushroom pan gravy. Heat 2 tablespoons oil in a large skillet or Dutch oven over medium-high heat. When the oil is hot, add the mushrooms and cook, stirring occasionally, until the liquid that the mushrooms release has completely evaporated and the mushrooms are beginning to caramelize, 7 to 8 minutes. Add the shallot and season with 1 teaspoon salt. Cook for another minute, stirring occasionally, then add the thyme and cook for 1 minute more. Stir in the wine and use a wooden spoon to deglaze the pan by scraping up any browned bits on the bottom. Let the wine reduce by half, about 2 minutes. Add the stock, bring to a boil, and cook until the mixture is reduced by a quarter, 4 to 5 minutes. Add the butter, stirring as it melts to emulsify. Let simmer for 3 minutes. Season to taste with additional salt.

You have two options: You can slice the meatloaf and serve it after it has rested, or, if you have time to spare, make the meatloaf 1 day in advance. When you are ready to serve, remove it from the pan and slice it into 8 pieces. Heat a cast-iron skillet over medium-high heat. Add 1 tablespoon oil, then add 2 slices of meatloaf and sear, turning once, until they are dark brown on both sides. Transfer to a plate and repeat with the remaining slices. Top with gravy and serve.

note: This recipe also works beautifully for meatballs.

Lamb was always a very special-occasion meal in my house growing up, and it was the centerpiece of every Easter Sunday. I think it still occupies that status for many home cooks. So one reason I adore lamb blade steak* is because it kicks over the pedestal, making lamb into an everyday affair. (Much of the food at Poole's operates on this philosophy.)

That said, this preparation has all the trappings of the leg of lamb my mother made every Easter, right down to the sauce. Just before we sat down at the table to eat, my mom would go out to the yard with scissors to harvest some of our highly invasive mint crop. She'd make a cider vinegar–based simple syrup, and just as she cut the heat off, she'd throw in a huge handful of the fresh mint. The entire house would fill with its perfume. Adding baking soda is an old trick to neutralize the astringency of the vinegar without losing its nice acidic kick.

The sauce offers the perfect juxtaposition to the rich gaminess of lamb and highlights everything that is wrong with the unnaturally green mint jelly on supermarket shelves. It's bright and fresh, and it brings a bit of occasion to the everyday.

Always be nice to your butcher so that when you need to, you can ask him or her to cut your lamb shoulder steaks with the riblets and eye bone intact. **SERVES 4**

4 (1-inch-thick) lamb shoulder steaks with riblets and eye bone (about 1¾ pounds)

2 teaspoons Poole's Cure (page 17)

½ cup sugar

⅔ cup cider vinegar

½ cup tightly packed chopped fresh mint

⅛ teaspoon baking soda

¼ cup peanuts, crushed

Sea salt

Black pepper in a mill

Continued

On a baking sheet, rub each steak all over with ½ teaspoon of the cure. Transfer to the refrigerator, uncovered, and let cure for 3 to 6 hours. One hour before cooking, take the steaks out of the refrigerator to come to room temperature.

Meanwhile, combine the sugar and vinegar in a small saucepan. Bring to a boil and cook for 2 minutes. Add the mint, remove from the heat, and stir in the baking soda. Let cool to room temperature.

Heat a small skillet over high heat until it's very hot. Add the crushed peanuts and immediately remove the skillet from the heat. Toss the peanuts in the skillet for 1 minute to toast. Season with ⅛ teaspoon salt.

Rinse the steaks and pat dry. Season the steaks with salt and a few cranks of pepper on both sides. In a large cast-iron skillet over medium-high heat, warm the oil. Add the steaks to the pan and nestle the halved garlic heads, cut side down, in the pan along with the sprigs of

1 tablespoon neutral vegetable oil

2 heads garlic, halved across
the equator

4 (2-inch) rosemary sprigs

2 tablespoons unsalted butter

rosemary. Sear for 1 minute, add the butter, and sear for an additional 90 seconds. Check the underside of one steak; it should be nicely browned. If so, flip the steaks (if not, cook for an additional 30 seconds). Move the rosemary and garlic to the tops of the steaks. Begin to baste the steaks by tilting the pan and using a spoon to gather the juices and pour over the steaks. Cook for another 2½ minutes, or until medium-rare (120°F on an instant thermometer inserted in the center of the steak), basting the steaks every 30 seconds.

Remove from the heat and baste for 2 more minutes. Transfer the steaks to individual plates and let rest for 10 minutes. To serve, drizzle 1 tablespoon of the mint vinegar over each steak and garnish with 1 tablespoon of the crushed peanuts. You can also spoon some of the pan drippings over the steak if you're so inclined. Serve with additional mint vinegar on the side.

Pan-Roasted Salmon with Spring Pistou

Salmon is one of the more misunderstood fish out there. You'll hear a lot of people say they hate salmon. *Hate* is such a strong word, but if you've ever had poor-quality farm-raised salmon, you can understand why people might throw that word around.

In season, Pacific wild salmon is a thing of beauty, however, and a far cry from any farm-raised version. It's rich and almost fruit-like in its sweetness. Brining the fish briefly locks in its silkiness and imparts seasoning throughout the fillet. I keep the brine simple to allow the salmon's complex and delicious personality to come through.

The *pistou* is bright, green, and herbaceous, like a classic pesto but without the weight. Pair this dish with the Creamy Rice Grits on page 181 for an amazing spring dinner. **SERVES 4**

½ cup kosher salt

2 cups ice

4 (6-ounce) wild salmon fillets, skin on, pin bones removed

Sea salt

TOMATO RELISH

1 cup halved cherry tomatoes

1 tablespoon minced shallots

Sea salt

2 tablespoons olive oil

PISTOU

½ cup olive oil

2 cloves garlic, minced

1 cup packed fresh basil leaves

Sea salt

2 tablespoons neutral vegetable oil

2 shallots, minced

2 cups white wine

1 cup clam juice

Continued

First, brine the salmon. In a large bowl, combine the kosher salt and 4 cups cold water. Stir to dissolve the salt. Add the ice and the salmon fillets and brine for 15 minutes. Transfer the fillets to a plate and pat dry. Score the skin side horizontally once across the middle of each fillet, taking care to make the incision shallow enough that you only score the skin and not the flesh.

To make the relish, combine the tomatoes and shallots in a small bowl. Season to taste with salt, then stir in the olive oil and set aside.

To make the pistou, in a food processor, puree the olive oil with the garlic. Add the basil leaves and 1 teaspoon salt and process until smooth. Transfer to a small bowl and store in the refrigerator until ready to finish.

In a large skillet over medium heat, swirl the oil to coat the pan. When the oil is shimmering, add the shallots and cook, stirring until they are softened, about 5 minutes. Pour in the wine and stir to scrape up any browned bits on the bottom of the pan. Bring the mixture to a boil, then reduce to a simmer. Cook until the mixture has reduced by a quarter, 3½ to 4 minutes. Stir in the clam juice and keep warm over low heat.

To finish the dish, place a large skillet over medium-high heat. Lightly season the fillets with salt. Heat the oil in the pan. When it shimmers, add the fillets, skin side down. Sear the fillets on one side; when they begin to brown slightly on the edges, after about 2½ minutes, add 1 tablespoon of the butter to the pan, tilting the pan around to help the butter melt and

2 tablespoons neutral vegetable oil

3 tablespoons cold unsalted butter, cut into cubes

Juice of ½ lemon

coat the pan's surface. Cook for another 3 minutes. Flip the fillets and let cook for 30 seconds. Then, tilting the pan slightly toward you, use a spoon to baste the fish by scooping up some of the butter and pouring it over the tops of the fillets. Continue to cook, basting with butter, for another 3 to 4 minutes, until the fish is just cooked through. Transfer to a baking sheet while you finish the pistou.

Heat the reserved clam juice mixture over high heat for 1 to 2 minutes, just until it is hot throughout and barely beginning to bubble. Remove from the heat, and whisk in the reserved basil puree. Add the remaining 2 tablespoons of butter and the lemon juice and season with salt to taste.

To serve, divide the fillets among four plates and pour some of the pistou sauce around each fillet. Top with a spoonful of the tomato relish and serve.

Fried Soft-Shell Crabs

In North Carolina, we're lucky to have a long soft-shell crab season. The first ones show up in late spring and they come in all summer long, until about October. Raleigh is about two hours from the coast, and we get our crabs about three hours after they've come of the water, thanks to Smiley, our crab runner. Smiley spends the warm months of the year shuttling back and forth from the ports to the restaurants in an old refrigerated truck with the word *seafood* hand-painted on the side.

The choosing of your soft shells is just as important as (if not more important than) the process of cooking them. The magic of soft shells is in tasting the waters from which they were pulled in every bite of tender meat, and the key to capturing this effect is in getting crabs that are still alive when you start cooking. Frozen soft shells just can't compare.

At Poole's we've started serving fried soft shells "top hat" style, a technique that Smiley passed on to us from his crab-fishing pals. By separating the top piece of shell from the rest of the body and frying it separately, you get a better crispy-shell-to-meat ratio. I like to serve them with a small pile of slaw stuffed between the pieces, sandwich-style.

It's also typical to order the soft shell at Poole's and have it arrive at the table with one of its tiny back legs missing. It's a line-cook trick to pull one of the small legs after frying to taste for seasoning; depending on the salinity of the water they were in, the soft shells may not need any additional salt whatsoever. Normally guests dig into the crab before pausing to count the legs and we get away with the tiny steal, but one night two of our regulars, Dan and Rusty, called me over and said, with a smile: "We want you to know that we know how many legs a crab has." Busted. **SERVES 4**

Continued

To clean the crabs, hold one in your hand and with the other hand snip off the front (face) of the crab with a pair of scissors, cutting about ¼ inch behind the eyes and mouth (this is the move that kills them, so be bold and merciful). Fold one of the "wings" of the top shell back and snip out the gills (they look like little white fingers that hang on either side). Repeat on the other side. Flip the crab over and pull off the apron (the

4 live soft shell crabs

4 cups buttermilk

4 cups all-purpose flour

2 tablespoons sea salt

1 tablespoon freshly ground
     black pepper

Neutral vegetable oil, for frying

1 cup Malted Slaw with Roasted
     Tomatoes (page 165)

darker-colored strip on the belly of the crab) as if you're pulling the tab on a can. Finally, turn the crab back over and flip up both sides of the top shell of the crab; it will be connected to the body lengthwise along the center. Then use your scissors to cut along the connective center so that you disconnect the top shell from the body of the crab. Set the crab pieces aside.

Pour the buttermilk into a shallow bowl. In a second shallow bowl, whisk together the flour, salt, and pepper.

Line a large plate with paper towels and set near the stove. Fill a large Dutch oven or heavy-bottomed pot halfway with oil and heat over medium-high heat until the oil reaches 350°F on a deep-fry thermometer. Dip the crab bodies into the buttermilk, followed by the flour mixture, making sure to coat completely. Set on a baking sheet. Repeat with the top shells.

Gently add the crab bodies to the oil in batches and fry until golden brown and crispy, about 6 minutes, flipping every few minutes. Transfer to a paper towel–lined plate. Pull off one of the small legs and taste to check the seasoning. Season with salt if desired.

Add the top shells to the oil and fry just until crispy, about 4 minutes. Transfer to the plate with the crab bodies.

To assemble, place a crab body on a plate and scoop a hefty spoonful of slaw onto the top of the crab. Top with one of the crab tops. Serve immediately.

Butter-Seared Octopus

Some of the very best octopus in the world is on the menu of City House in Nashville, Tennessee. After devouring it on every visit and marveling at its brilliantly tender texture and perfectly seasoned flavor, I finally asked the chef, my friend Tandy Wilson, for his secret. "Wine corks," he said, then explained that he always adds a few wine corks to the braising liquid in which he cooks the octopus. I gave him a stupefied side-eye, wondering if he was pulling one over on me. But when I got home, I gave it try and have been doing it ever since.

Though the corks don't have a scientifically explainable effect on how the octopus cooks, there's a romance to the idea of this method that, to me, gets at the heart of what I love about cooking. Technique and the recipes aside, being in the kitchen is an intuitive, intoxicating dance. And not fully understanding the whys behind every move heightens the feeling of giddy wonder that occurs when you're eating a dish you've made for the first time.

If you're intimidated by cooking octopus at home, don't be. Octopus is becoming more widely available (the Whole Foods near my house now carries fresh octopus), and it is far easier to prepare than you might think. For the corks, use those made of traditional natural cork, not synthetic or compressed ones. I like to serve this octopus on top of a scoop of butter beans and Marinated Peppers (page 230), and garnished with cornbread crumbs (see page 100). **SERVES 6 to 8**

1 (7- to 8-pound) whole octopus (if using frozen, let thaw completely overnight)

Kosher salt

1 bunch celery, coarsely chopped

2 heads garlic, halved across the equator

2 fresh bay leaves

10 thyme sprigs

4 wine corks

1 tablespoon neutral vegetable oil

Continued

In a large stockpot, combine 10 quarts water, ¼ cup kosher salt, and the celery, garlic, bay leaves, and thyme. Bring the water to a boil, then reduce to a simmer. Add the corks and then lower the octopus into the liquid. Return to a simmer and cook the octopus for 45 minutes to 1 hour, until tender. Make sure that the octopus is completely submerged in the liquid, adding more water if necessary to keep the octopus covered. Remove from the heat and let the octopus cool down to room temperature in the braising liquid (again, making sure that the octopus is completely submerged).

Remove the octopus from the liquid, pausing to let excess liquid drain back into the pot, and place it on a cutting board; discard the braising liquid. Slice the head off and discard. Now you have to remove the beak (far easier than it sounds!). Flip the octopus over so that you're looking at

1 tablespoon unsalted butter

Lemon, for squeezing

the center where all its legs meet: you'll see a sharp triangular piece that looks like a bird's beak (it's often black or dark in color). Use a paring knife to cut a small circle around the beak, then pop it out (almost like coring a tomato) and discard. Cut the tentacles and body into 2-inch pieces, slicing on the diagonal. (You can prepare the octopus to this point up to 1 day ahead; cover and refrigerate, then let the octopus come up to room temperature for 1 hour before proceeding with searing.)

Heat a skillet over medium-high heat with the oil. When the oil is very hot, add the octopus pieces and sear for about 1 minute. Add the butter and continue to cook, stirring frequently and using a spoon to baste the octopus in the butter, until the pieces are crispy and caramelized, 5 minutes.

Divide the octopus among plates, squeeze the lemon over the top of the octopus and serve.

Braised Pork Shanks

It's not uncommon to hear that meat cooked on the bone has more flavor, and the pork shank is the perfect defense for that thesis.

By braising shanks, you get two for one: beautiful, tender confit-like protein, and a braising liquid with richness that would be hard to replicate with the standard path of just bones, aromatics, and a stock pot. This wouldn't be possible if it weren't for the perfectly aligned relationship between meat and bone that naturally occurs with the shank.

Serving the shanks classically on the bone has a show-stopping effect, and makes a beautiful centerpiece to a celebratory meal. But meat is also excellent when pulled and served alongside (or over the top of) vegetables. Pull the meat into large nobs, reheat them in the leftover braising liquid, and serve with Pit Peas (page 141) or Stewed Tomatoes (page 142). Or cut the meat into bite-size pieces and use it as the anchor of the pork and dumplings on page 186. However you treat this dish, do not waste the beautiful braising liquid. Any leftovers should be reserved (they can be frozen for up to 6 months); use them to make a quick pan sauce or gravy, or as the base of a stew. **SERVES 4**

4 pork shanks (about 5 pounds total)

4 tablespoons Poole's Cure (page 17)

Sea salt

Black pepper in a mill

2 tablespoons neutral vegetable oil

1 yellow onion, cut into eighths

2 heads garlic, halved along the equator

1½ cups carrots (from about 4 medium carrots), roughly chopped

1½ cups celery (from about 4 stalks celery), roughly chopped

1½ teaspoons black peppercorns

2 fresh bay leaves, torn

8 medium thyme sprigs

Rub each pork shank with 1 tablespoon of the cure. Place on a rimmed baking sheet, wrap with plastic wrap, and transfer to the refrigerator and chill for 12 hours.

Preheat a convection oven to 300°F (or a regular oven to 325°F). Rinse the shanks and pat dry. Season lightly with salt and freshly ground black pepper. In a 9½-quart Dutch oven over medium-high heat, warm the oil until it shimmers. Add the shanks in an even layer. Brown the shanks on all sides, 5 to 6 minutes per side. Watch carefully; the sugar in the cure can burn, so adjust the heat if the shanks begin to darken too quickly in spots. You're looking for a nice light brown crust on the shanks. Transfer to a baking sheet and set aside.

Add the onion and garlic, cut side down, to the Dutch oven and cook, stirring occasionally, until they are caramelized, about 10 minutes. Add the carrot, celery, peppercorns, bay, and thyme, and cook, stirring occasionally, for 5 minutes, until the vegetables are slightly softened. Add the wine and scrape the bottom of the pan with a wooden spoon to release any caramelized bits.

1 (750-ml) bottle white wine

2 tablespoons Roasted Garlic Butter (page 20)

Return the shanks to the pan, add 8 cups water, and stir to combine and coat the shanks. Increase the heat to high. Bring to a boil, then reduce to a simmer. Cover the Dutch oven and transfer to the oven; cook for 3 hours, until the meat is tender and offers no resistance when pierced with a knife.

Cool the shanks in the braising liquid until cool enough to handle, about 30 minutes. Transfer the shanks to a baking sheet and cover with foil while you make the sauce (see Note). Strain the braising liquid (you should have about 6 to 7 cups) and discard the solids. Bring the liquid to a simmer and reduce by half. Remove from heat and stir in the garlic butter. Season with salt to taste. Arrange the shanks on a platter and top with a few spoons of the sauce. Serve with additional sauce on the side.

note: If you're serving the shanks on the bone, this makes 4 very generous (10 ounces of meat per person) portions. You could also pull the meat and serve over vegetables to easily serve 6 to 8.

If you're making the shanks ahead and using the meat for another recipe (such as the pork and dumplings on page 186, for example), do not reduce the braising liquid. Strain it and reserve to add flavor back to the final dish.

Desserts

Poole's opened in its first incarnation in 1945 as Poole's Pie Shop. Guests still come in telling tales of the delicious handmade pies, in every flavor you can imagine, that used to line the counters.

We kicked off our first dessert menu at Poole's with a commitment to serve only pies, in tribute to the original use of the space. Spliced between the million other items on the prep list, Sunny and I would bake pies (he made the crust and I made the fillings). What we hadn't considered was the guest who would say, "What else do you have? I don't like pie." (Side note: How does one not like pie?!) But then, we also got antsy and wondered about paying tribute to the other comfort-food classics. Where would the hummingbird cake go? Or the doughnuts, or the dark chocolate *pots de crème*?

Ultimately, we caved to our own restlessness and expanded our dessert list. We made layer cakes, generally iced during the first thirty minutes of service while they were still barely warm. We cobbled together cookie recipes, crafting hybrids from our favorites and filling them with cocoa nibs and coffee beans so we could call them our own. We were line cooks at heart, so all of the desserts were properly salted and never oversweetened. At the time, we never served my one dessert vice, ice cream. Who has time to make ice cream? Or to buy an ice cream maker? I chuckle thinking about the off-road nature of our dessert approach back then, but damn, it was fun. And it was truly delicious, and full of heart.

As the company grew up, we eventually hired an executive pastry chef to manage a team to produce pastry (and now breads) for all of our restaurants (there are currently seven). Poole's has always had a bit of a Wild West habit of doing whatever is necessary, so the change was bittersweet. That said, we needed a special sugar boss. Enter Andrew Ullom.

It's amazing to work with such spirited talent as Andrew. We knew that our approach to desserts (like most of what we did at the time) was by-the-seat-of-our-pants-crazy, but it was ours, and we loved it. Adding a new contributor to that spontaneous program felt kind of like your mom getting remarried when you were just fine after the divorce. But Andrew turned out to be the super-rad stepbrother you always wanted. He loved and respected what we loved and respected; it was like he had been there all along. He's helped us reinvent all of those scratched-up Poole's Diner classics, and we've gone on a number of new family adventures since he arrived.

On a regular night at home, I'm not the biggest dessert person. A spoonful or two of ice cream is really all I need to satisfy a somewhat dormant sweet tooth. But I love a full dessert table on special occasions: Thanksgiving isn't complete without at least four types of pie. The desserts in this chapter run the gamut from more involved special-occasion desserts (like my favorite coconut cream pie on page 255) to simpler recipes that can be put together on a weekday (like bumbleberry crisp on page 262).

Sweet Potato Hummingbird Cake

There's a debate that rages in all corners of the dessert-eating universe: cake or pie? It's of particular importance in the South, where both tall-as-the-sky layer cakes and blue-ribbon pies are matters of pride and heritage. Though Poole's has pie in its blood, we could never get away with omitting cake from the lineup.

This occasion-worthy cake is based on a classic hummingbird cake. First published in *Southern Living* magazine in 1978, the original version, created by Mrs. L. H. Wiggins of Greensboro, North Carolina, the city where I was born, had banana and pineapple in its batter. It has since become one of the most requested recipes in the magazine's history.

Our version adds sweet potatoes to the mix and substitutes green peanuts for the traditional pecans. Green, or "raw," peanuts aren't roasted like the peanuts at a baseball game, and they have a tender, almost bean-like texture. They're worth seeking out (they come into season in the late summer and fall), but if you can't find them near you, feel free to use roasted peanuts or another nut of your choice. We roast the bananas before adding them to the cake batter for two reasons: it concentrates the flavors of the banana and it yields a particularly smooth puree, which is better for the texture of the cake. Roasted banana puree will keep in the freezer in a resealable plastic bag for up to 6 months. **MAKES one 9-inch cake**

4 bananas

4½ cups all-purpose flour

1½ teaspoons baking soda

1½ teaspoons sea salt

2 cups sugar

¾ teaspoon ground cinnamon

5 large eggs

2 cups neutral vegetable oil

3 cups diced pineapple

1 tablespoon pure vanilla extract

1 cup dried black currants

Continued

Preheat a convection oven to 400°F (or a regular oven to 425°F). Arrange the bananas (in their peels) on a parchment-lined baking sheet and bake in the oven until they are black and slightly deflated, about 25 minutes. Let the bananas cool to room temperature. Remove the peels and discard and transfer the banana flesh and any juices that collected on the pan to a food processor. Process until smooth. Measure 2 cups of the puree and set aside (reserve any extra puree for another use).

Reduce the oven temperature to 325°F convection (350°F regular). Spray three 9-inch cake pans with nonstick cooking spray and line with parchment. In a large bowl, mix together the flour, baking soda, salt, sugar, and cinnamon.

In a medium bowl, whisk together the eggs, oil, and banana puree until well combined. Fold in the pineapple, vanilla, currants, and peanuts.

2 cups green peanuts

2 pounds sweet potatoes, peeled
(about 3 medium)

ICING

2 (8-ounce) packages cream
cheese, at room temperature

2 cups unsalted butter,
at room temperature

3¾ cups confectioners' sugar

1 teaspoon sea salt

1 teaspoon pure vanilla extract

2 cups roasted peanuts, roughly
chopped, for garnish

Grate the sweet potatoes on the large holes of a box grater and fold into the wet mixture.

Pour the wet ingredients into the bowl with the flour mixture and stir with a rubber spatula until just incorporated. Divide the batter equally among the three pans and bake until firm and golden brown, 45 to 50 minutes. Let the cakes cool for 10 minutes in the pans on wire racks, then turn out onto the racks, peel off the parchment, and let cool completely.

Meanwhile, make the icing. In the bowl of a stand mixer fitted with the paddle attachment, mix the cream cheese until smooth. Add the butter and mix on low speed, stopping occasionally to scrape down the sides of the bowl. With the mixer running on low speed, add the sugar by the ½ cup until it's fully incorporated. Add the salt and vanilla and mix to combine.

To assemble the cake, use a serrated knife to trim the top of each layer to make sure it's flat (reserve the trimmings for snacking). Place a cake layer on a platter or cake stand. Using an offset spatula, spread 1½ cups of the icing over the first layer. Top with a second layer and repeat with 1½ cups of the icing. Top with the third layer and use the remaining icing to frost the top and sides of the cake. Press the roasted peanuts up onto the sides of the cake for garnish.

The cake, once assembled, can be stored, covered, in the refrigerator for 2 to 3 days, but it's best the day it's made. Serve at room temperature.

I'm a sucker for coconut cream pie. This is the version from Poole's, which we enrich with good coconut milk and cream. It also has a macadamia nut shortbread cookie crust that's over-the-top delicious. It's on my "last meal" list.

Truthfully, this recipe is complicated, but all of the steps can be done up to three days in advance and stored until you're ready to serve (and it's best to start at least one day before serving, as the coconut custard needs to be refrigerated for several hours). In addition to coconut milk, the custard is enriched with coconut cream, which has less water than coconut milk and helps the custard set up almost like it has gelatin. You can find coconut cream at most Asian markets or even at Trader Joe's. Don't make the mistake of buying sweetened cream of coconut (aka Coco López), which you'd use to make a piña colada; one is not like the other. Finally, we use fresh coconut that we toast and then fold into the pie. I absolutely love the flavor of fresh coconut, but I also get that hacking a melon-size fruit open with a knife isn't for everyone, so feel free to substitute good-quality unsweetened coconut flakes if you like. **MAKES one 9-inch pie**

SHORTBREAD CRUST

¼ cup macadamia nuts

1¼ cups all-purpose flour

¼ cup sugar

½ teaspoon sea salt

½ cup ice-cold unsalted butter,
  cut into ½-inch cubes

1 large egg yolk

1 teaspoon pure vanilla extract

1 tablespoon ice water

Continued

To make the crust, pulse the nuts with ½ cup of the flour in a food processor until even-size crumbs form. Add the remaining flour and sugar and pulse to combine. Add the salt and butter and pulse until the butter forms pea-size pieces.

In a small bowl, whisk together the egg yolk, vanilla, and ice water. Slowly drizzle the egg mixture into the food processor while pulsing. As soon as the dough has mostly come together, turn it out onto an 18-inch-long piece of plastic wrap. Press the dough into a 1-inch-thick round. Wrap tightly with the plastic and smooth out the dough by rolling a rolling pin over the plastic wrap a few times. Refrigerate for 1 hour or overnight.

Remove the dough from the refrigerator, unwrap, and place on a lightly floured surface (or on a large sheet of wax paper). Roll the dough out to a round ⅛-inch thick, about 10 inches wide, and transfer to a 9-inch pie plate. Trim the excess to an overhang of ½ inch and crimp the edge as

COCONUT FILLING

1 young coconut (or 3 cups unsweetened coconut flakes)

2 cups coconut cream

¾ cup plus 2 tablespoons coconut milk, plus 6 to 8 tablespoons more if needed to thin custard

6 large egg yolks

½ cup sugar

¼ cup cornstarch

1 tablespoon unsalted butter

Soft whipped cream, for serving

desired. Place the crust in the freezer for 1 hour. (Save the scraps in case you need to patch any holes in the crust.)

Preheat a convection oven to 375°F (or a regular oven to 400°F). Line the piecrust with parchment paper and fill with dried beans or pie weights. Bake for 30 minutes and remove the weights and parchment and lower the oven temperature to 300°F convection (325°F regular); bake for another 10 to 15 minutes, until golden brown. Let cool completely. (The crust can be wrapped in plastic wrap and stored at room temperature for 1 day.)

To make the filling, first prepare the coconut. Use the heel of a large knife to make incisions in a circle around the coconut from top to bottom, until the coconut starts to split and release coconut water. (You want to tap the coconut from pole to pole, not around the equator; doing it this way makes it much easier to remove the meat.) Pull the coconut apart and drain the coconut water (save it for another use). Run a butter knife between the meat and the husk to loosen. Pull the meat from the husk and shave it into strips with a Y-peeler. Arrange the coconut meat in an even layer on a baking sheet and roast, stirring halfway through, for 5 to 8 minutes, until it's starting to turn golden brown.

In a medium saucepan over medium heat, combine the coconut cream, ¾ cup plus 2 tablespoons of the coconut milk, and 2 cups of the roasted coconut and cook until hot but not boiling. In a medium bowl, whisk together the egg yolks, sugar, cornstarch, and salt until smooth and pale in color. While whisking, add 1 cup of the cream mixture, 1 tablespoon at a time, to the egg mixture. (This tempers the eggs and keeps them from curdling.) Whisk in the remaining cream mixture, then return it all to the saucepan and cook over medium heat, whisking constantly, until the custard thickens and reaches between 178°F and 185°F on an instant thermometer. Remove from the heat and stir in the butter until melted and smooth. Strain the custard through a fine-mesh sieve set over a plastic container. Cover the custard with plastic wrap, pressing it directly onto the surface to prevent a film from forming. Refrigerate for at least 4 hours, or overnight. (The custard can be made 2 to 3 days ahead.)

If you'd like the custard to be thinner, whisk as much of the extra coconut milk as needed to create the desired consistency. Fill the crust with the custard and refrigerate for 1 hour. Top with a heaping spoonful of whipped cream and garnish with the remaining roasted coconut strips.

Poole's Piecrust

Everybody has a preferred piecrust recipe, a preferred method. I'm not here to debate—if you have a piecrust recipe that you love, by all means, use it. But in our many years of making pie, we've come across a few super handy tricks.

If you have the time, it helps to roll out your piecrust, press it into a pie tin, wrap it in plastic wrap, and then let it sit in the freezer overnight. This will allow the gluten to fully relax and will keep it from shrinking or slouching when baked. Additionally, Andrew is a firm believer that you should bake a crust all the way through for any recipe that calls for a blind-baked (prebaked) shell. Doing so will make sure you never encounter that doughy not-completely-cooked top layer of crust. Just be sure to watch the edges of your crust on a second bake, and cover it with foil if it starts to darken too much. **MAKES four 9-inch piecrusts**

2 cups unsalted butter, cut into ½-inch cubes

5½ cups all-purpose flour

4 teaspoons sugar

1 teaspoon kosher salt

⅔ cup ice water

note: If you're going to the trouble of making piecrust from scratch, make a few extra (this recipe will make four). They keep beautifully in the freezer.

In a large bowl, combine the butter, flour, sugar, and salt. Place the bowl in the freezer for 30 minutes. Use two butter knives to cut the butter into the flour mixture until pea-size pieces form. Massage the butter pieces between your fingers, stretching them into thin ribbons.

Add the ice water to the flour by the tablespoon, stirring to combine. Add water only to the point that the dough holds together when pinched between your fingers; you may not need all of it. Gather the dough into a ball; divide into 4 equal pieces. Press each piece into a disk and wrap in plastic wrap. Refrigerate the dough for 1 hour.

On a well-floured work surface, roll out each piece of dough into a round 11 inches wide and about ⅛ inch thick. Transfer each round to a pie tin; trim the overhang to ½ inch and crimp as desired. Wrap each tin in plastic wrap and freeze overnight (the frozen pie shells will keep, frozen, for up to 6 months). When ready to bake, preheat a convection oven to 325°F (or a regular oven to 350°F). Line the shell with parchment paper and fill with pie weights (dry beans or rice works great). Bake for 30 minutes. Remove the weights and parchment and bake another 15 minutes, or until the crust is cooked through and golden brown. Let cool on a rack and use as desired.

Dark Chocolate Pecan Pie

My mother makes the best pecan pie, and her "secret" started out as a mistake (as so many recipes do). For years, she had faithfully followed the recipe on the back of the Karo corn syrup bottle. Then, one Thanksgiving, she misread the amount of vanilla extract in the recipe and added 1 tablespoon instead of 1 teaspoon. That triple vanilla went a long way; the pie was extra fragrant and had a nutty richness that made sure everyone went in for seconds.

Out of respect to my mother's pie, we use Karo in our version too, with a few tweaks. Corn syrup is a maligned ingredient these days, so if you'd feel more comfortable using cane syrup, go for it. I have tried to cut corn syrup out of my diet where possible, and this pie is one exception—everything in moderation, right? The quality of the chocolate is key here: use the best you can find, preferably from a bean-to-bar operation. And don't skimp on the vanilla! **MAKES one 9-inch pie**

2 ounces dark chocolate (70 percent cacao), roughly chopped

3 large eggs

1 cup sugar

4 tablespoons unsalted butter, melted and cooled to room temperature

1 cup light corn syrup

1½ teaspoons pure vanilla extract

A pinch of sea salt

2 tablespoons bourbon (optional)

1½ cups chopped pecans

1 Poole's Piecrust (page 259), prebaked and cooled

Preheat a convection oven to 325°F (or a regular oven to 350°F).

Prepare a double boiler by setting a heatproof bowl over a medium saucepan filled with 1 inch of simmering water. Add the chocolate to the bowl and stir with a rubber spatula until melted and smooth. Let cool.

In a medium bowl, whisk together the eggs and sugar. Whisk in the melted butter, followed by the corn syrup, melted chocolate, vanilla extract, salt, and bourbon. Arrange the pecans in an even layer in the baked pie shell. Pour the filling over the pecans.

Transfer the pie to the oven and bake for about 1 hour, until it is set with just a slight jiggle when you shake it. (Watch the edges of the crust carefully and cover with foil if they start to darken considerably.) Let cool completely before serving.

Buttermilk Chess Pie with Grilled Peaches

Chess pie frequently falls into a class of desserts I define as "teeth-chatteringly sweet." With a filling made largely of eggs and sugar, chess pies were designed as a pantry dessert, something you could throw together with what you had on hand. I'm not the biggest fan of overly sweet desserts, but in the case of chess pie, that tooth tingle has a certain charm about it. Here, the addition of buttermilk and lemon helps restrain the sugar, balancing it out with welcome acidity.

The pie itself is evergreen: make it any time of year that suits you. I add grilled peaches in the summer because I can't help but incorporate fresh fruit into all desserts, but you could swap them out for another fruit or, in the winter, a preserve. **MAKES one 9-inch pie**

⅔ cup granulated sugar

¾ cup packed light brown sugar

2 teaspoons cornmeal

2 tablespoons all-purpose flour

¼ teaspoon sea salt, plus more for the peaches

2 large whole eggs

2 large egg yolks

½ cup unsalted melted butter, cooled to room temperature

⅔ cup buttermilk

Juice and zest of 1 lemon

½ teaspoon pure vanilla extract

1 Poole's Piecrust (page 259), prebaked and cooled

4 peaches, halved and pitted

4 to 6 tablespoons olive oil

Preheat a convection oven to 325°F (or a regular oven to 350°F).

In a large bowl, mix the sugars, cornmeal, flour, and salt together.

In another bowl, whisk the whole eggs and egg yolks together. Drizzle in the melted butter, whisking to combine. Add the buttermilk, lemon juice and zest, and vanilla and whisk to combine. Slowly whisk in the dry ingredients until just combined.

Pour the custard into the prebaked crust and bake until just set, 40 to 50 minutes. Watch the edges of the crust carefully and cover with foil if they start to darken considerably. Let cool for 1 hour.

While the pie is baking, prepare a charcoal grill. (Alternatively, you could use a grill pan or very hot cast-iron skillet.) Drizzle the cut sides of the peach halves with olive oil and sprinkle with sea salt. Grill the peaches, cut side down, until they are slightly charred, about 4 minutes. Turn the peaches over with tongs and cook for another 2 minutes. Let the peaches cool slightly; when they're cool enough to handle, coarsely chop (you can remove the peels beforehand if you prefer; personally, I hate peach skin). Transfer the peaches and any juices to a bowl.

To serve, top each slice of pie with a spoonful of the grilled peaches and their juices.

Bumbleberry Crisp with Lemon Curd

Before I knew that I wanted to cook as a career, I hosted a lot of dinner parties. What would start as ten guests would quickly grow to twenty . . . then thirty . . . even forty people who would somehow fit themselves into my modest college student's apartment. That meant that I'd be faced with the challenge of feeding four times as many friends as I had bought food for.

There are a handful of recipes that every cook should file away for such moments, recipes that will bend to the occasion with ease. Berry crisp is certainly one of them.

This free-form dessert couldn't be simpler: toss berries with sugar, bake with a crunchy top, and serve. And if unexpected guests arrive, simply add a few more cups of whatever berries you have on hand (the term *bumbleberry* was coined in the Northeast and refers to a mix of at least three berries). Whenever I make this recipe, I always make double the streusel and bake the second half like granola on a baking sheet. It's amazing sprinkled over ice cream or fruit salad. Our pastry chef, Andrew, has even been known to eat it with milk in a bowl for breakfast. It keeps for 1 week in a resealable plastic bag on the counter or up to 1 month in the freezer.

The lemon curd is a delicious counterpoint to the berries, but you could always swap in vanilla ice cream or soft whipped cream if you prefer. **SERVES 8 to 10**

LEMON CURD

¾ cup fresh lemon juice

4 teaspoons lemon zest

¼ teaspoon sea salt

8 egg yolks

1¼ cups granulated sugar

½ cup unsalted butter, cut
    into cubes

To make the curd, in a medium saucepan over low heat, warm the juice, zest, and salt. In a large bowl, whisk the egg yolks and granulated sugar until pale and smooth, about 2 minutes. Very slowly whisk the warm lemon juice mixture into the egg mixture until completely incorporated. Transfer the egg mixture back to the saucepan and place it over medium heat. Whisk ferociously (this incorporates air into the curd and makes it extra silky) until you see the very first bubble of a boil; continue to whisk like a maniac for 30 seconds, then remove the pan from the heat and stir in the butter, whisking until it completely melts and is incorporated.

Strain the curd through a fine-mesh sieve set over a container. Cover with plastic wrap, pressing it directly onto the surface of the curd to prevent a film from forming. Refrigerate for 1 hour before use. The curd can

Continued

OAT STREUSEL

1¼ cups rolled oats

2½ cups gluten-free or
 all-purpose flour

2¼ teaspoons cornstarch

13 tablespoons unsalted butter

½ teaspoon sea salt

½ teaspoon baking soda

½ teaspoon baking powder

to 221°F. Remove from the heat and let cool completely at room temperature. The cherries can be prepared up to 1 week in advance and stored in a lidded container in the refrigerator (you could also can these in mason jars using the hot water bath method and keep them up to 6 months).

To prepare the streusel, preheat a convection oven to 325°F (or a regular oven to 350°F). In a large bowl, mix the oats, flour, cornstarch, butter, salt, baking soda, and baking powder together with your hands until pea-size crumbs form. Spread the mixture on a baking sheet and bake for 12 to 15 minutes, until golden brown, stirring occasionally to keep it from browning unevenly. Let cool. The streusel will keep for 1 week in a resealable plastic bag on the counter.

To assemble, spoon some of the cherries on top of each ramekin of *panna cotta* and follow with a sprinkle of the streusel. Or, if you'd like to unmold the *panna cotta*, dip the bottoms of the ramekins in warm water for a few seconds, then run a knife around the perimeter. Flip the ramekins over onto serving plates and top with cherries and streusel.

One of the first recipes I ever attempted to cook by myself was beignets from a box of Café du Monde beignet mix. I was probably about seven or eight. My mother walked into the kitchen right around the time I was heating up a giant pot of oil, shrieked, and promptly shut down my doughnut operation. But my love for doughnuts lived on.

These zucchini fritters have a restrained sweetness, but if you'd like to amp up the sugar, add 1 teaspoon to the mascarpone you serve them with. **MAKES 20 to 30 golf ball–size doughnuts**

1½ cups shredded zucchini (from about 2 zucchini)

1¾ pounds Pâte à Choux (page 58)

1 tablespoon granulated sugar

Neutral vegetable oil, for frying

1 cup confectioners' sugar

2 cups mascarpone, for serving

Place the zucchini in the center of a large double-layer square of cheesecloth. Gather the edges together and carefully squeeze out as much excess liquid as you can. Set the zucchini aside.

Place the pâte à choux in a large bowl and fold in the zucchini and granulated sugar with a spatula. Cover the bowl with plastic wrap and chill the dough in the refrigerator for 2 hours.

Line a platter with several layers of paper towels. Fill a heavy-bottomed pot or Dutch oven halfway full with oil and heat over medium-high heat until it reaches 330°F on a deep-fry thermometer. Scoop 10 to 12 tablespoon-size portions of the batter into the oil. Fry the doughnuts until they're golden on one side, about 4 minutes. Flip the doughnuts and fry for 3 minutes more, until they are golden brown on all sides. Test for doneness by transferring one doughnut to the paper towel–lined platter and break it open to check it; the inside should be custardy but not raw. Transfer all of the doughnuts in the batch to the platter. Repeat with the remaining batter in batches until all of the batter is used.

Let the last batch of doughnuts cool slightly, then sift confectioners' sugar over all of the doughnuts. Serve alongside the mascarpone. Instruct your guests to tear open the doughnuts and slather with some of the mascarpone.

Jacked Up Devil's Food Trifle

Pudding is such a simple yet brilliant way to showcase chocolate. To me, it has the elegance of mousse or *pot de crème* without the formality— like a debutante kicking off her heels at the end of the night.

The pudding in this trifle will only be as good as the chocolate you buy, so use it as an excuse to pick your favorite (and snack on any extra). We use Videri chocolate, which is made in a bean-to-bar factory just on the other side of the railroad tracks from Poole's. **SERVES 12**

CHOCOLATE PUDDING

1½ cups sugar

½ teaspoon sea salt

3 cups milk

1 pound milk chocolate, chopped

2 vanilla beans, split, scraped and pod coarsely chopped

12 large egg yolks

4 cups heavy cream

6 tablespoons cornstarch

CAKE

3 cups all-purpose flour

2 cups Dutch-processed cocoa powder

2½ teaspoons baking soda

2½ teaspoons baking powder

¼ teaspoon kosher salt

1 cup milk

4 ounces espresso or brewed coffee, warm

4 large eggs

2¼ cups sugar

1½ cups olive oil

4 cups heavy cream, whipped to stiff peaks

Continued

To make the pudding, in a large saucepan over medium heat, combine the sugar, salt, milk, chocolate, and vanilla seeds and pod. Heat, whisking constantly, until the mixture reaches 180°F on an instant thermometer, about 10 minutes. Remove from heat.

In a large bowl, whisk the egg yolks and heavy cream together. Whisking constantly, add 1 cup of the hot chocolate mixture 1 tablespoon at a time; this tempers the eggs and keeps them from curdling. Whisk in the remaining chocolate mixture until fully combined.

In a small bowl, mix the cornstarch and ½ cup water to form a slurry, whisking well to make sure no lumps form. Add to the chocolate custard mixture and whisk well to combine.

Return the chocolate custard mixture to the saucepan and cook over medium-low heat, stirring constantly, until it reaches 180°F on an instant thermometer. Strain the pudding through a fine-mesh sieve set over a bowl. Press a piece of plastic wrap directly onto the surface to keep a film from forming. Refrigerate for at least 4 hours and ideally overnight.

To make the cake, preheat a convection oven to 325°F (or a regular oven to 350°F). Spray two 13-by-9-inch baking dishes with nonstick cooking spray. Line the bottom of each baking dish with parchment.

In a large bowl, sift together the flour, cocoa, baking soda, baking powder, and salt. In a small bowl, stir together the milk and espresso.

In the bowl of a stand mixer fitted with the paddle attachment, mix the eggs and sugar on medium speed until the mixture turns a pale yellow and the paddle forms ribbons when you raise it from the surface of the mixture. With the mixer running, add the olive oil in a slow stream until thoroughly incorporated. Turn off the mixer and scrape down the sides of the bowl with a rubber spatula.

With the mixer on low speed, add one-third of the flour mixture; when it's almost combined, add half of the espresso mixture. Repeat with the second third of the flour mixture and the rest of the espresso mixture. Add the last of the flour mixture and stop the mixer when it's almost (but not completely) incorporated.

Divide the cake batter evenly between the prepared baking dishes and bake for 18 to 20 minutes, rotating the dishes 180 degrees halfway through cooking. Let the cakes cool to room temperature. Break up each cake into bite-size crumbles and set aside.

To assemble the trifle, spoon half of the pudding into a 4-quart trifle dish in an even layer. Follow with one-third of the whipped cream, spreading it in an even layer. Top with half the cake crumbles, pressing them into a flat, even layer. Repeat with the second half of the pudding, followed by the second one-third of the whipped cream, followed by the remaining cake crumbles. Top with the final third of the whipped cream. Refrigerate for at least 1 hour (and up to 6 hours) before serving. To serve, spoon heaping dollops of the trifle onto plates, making sure to get some of each layer.

Our pastry chef, Andrew, is a pretty accomplished gardener, which means he's also very enthusiastic about "putting up," whether it's making pickles, preserves, or vinegars—anything to give fresh fruit and vegetables more longevity in the kitchen.

Strawberries and rhubarb both have short seasons here, so turning the rhubarb into marmalade gives us a little bit more time to enjoy this pairing. Use bruised and maybe slightly overripe strawberries; by macerating them in sugar they get to shine. Biscuits anchor the dessert (another reason why the marmalade works so well), but even those don't have to be fresh from the oven. If you have day-old biscuits (or cornbread) lying around, toast a few in brown butter, and proceed with the rest of the recipe. **SERVES 12; makes 2 cups marmalade**

BISCUITS

2 cups self-rising flour

2 tablespoons coarse
  yellow cornmeal

¼ cup sugar

¾ teaspoon kosher salt

½ cup cold unsalted butter

1 cup buttermilk

MARMALADE

2½ cups chopped rhubarb

1⅓ cups sugar

¼ cup champagne vinegar

Pinch of sea salt

Juice and zest of ½ lemon

1½ pounds strawberries, hulled

¼ cup sugar

Pinch of sea salt

Whipped cream, for serving

To make the biscuits, in a large bowl, whisk together the flour, cornmeal, sugar, and salt. Grate the cold butter on the large holes of a box grater over the bowl of dry ingredients. Mix with your hands, breaking up any clumps of butter. Refrigerate for at least an hour.

Preheat a convection oven to 400°F (or a regular oven to 425°F).

Add the buttermilk to the flour mixture and mix until just incorporated. On a heavily floured surface, roll the biscuit mixture into an 8-by-12-inch rectangle. Cut it into 2-inch squares.

Arrange the squares on a baking sheet, close enough to be almost touching. Bake for 15 to 16 minutes, rotating the pan halfway through, until the biscuits are dark golden brown on top.

To make the marmalade, in a saucepan over medium-low heat, combine the rhubarb, sugar, vinegar, salt, and lemon juice and zest. Cook, stirring occasionally, until the mixture thickens into a stew with some chunks remaining, 20 to 30 minutes. Let cool.

Slice the strawberries into bite-size pieces. Place in a bowl and toss with the sugar and salt; cover and let sit for 20 to 30 minutes.

To serve, pour a spoonful of marmalade onto a plate. Slice a biscuit in half diagonally and place half on top of the marmalade. Top it with a spoonful of the strawberries, then place the other biscuit half on top of that; top with more strawberries. Finish with a scoop of whipped cream.

Chocolate Chip Cookies and Milk

One of our frequent flyers on the dessert menu at Poole's is a plate of warm chocolate chip cookies served with a glass of milk. Far more intimate and friendly than the typical cookie plate arrangements that plague some dessert menus, our chocolate chip cookies are faithful and honest versions of the ones you grew up on. Rather than fall into the chewy or crunchy camps, this version is diplomatic—the edges take on a crunchy bite while the center stays tender and chewy. There are two technical elements to achieving this. First, mix the dough just a bit less than you think you should at each turn. It's absolutely okay if there are still bits of unincorporated flour in your final dough. Second, shape the cookie dough, refrigerate overnight, and then bake straight from the refrigerator. **MAKES about 20 cookies**

2¼ cups all-purpose flour

¾ teaspoon sea salt

1¼ teaspoons baking soda

1¼ cups unsalted butter

1 cup granulated sugar

½ cup plus 2 tablespoons packed light brown sugar

2 large eggs

1½ teaspoons pure vanilla extract

2½ cups chocolate chips

Milk, for serving

Sift the flour, salt, and baking soda into a medium bowl. In a stand mixer fitted with the paddle attachment, mix the butter and sugars together on medium speed until barely combined. Add the eggs and vanilla and mix until partly combined. Add the sifted dry ingredients and mix until the batter is lumpy but not completely combined. Add the chocolate chips and mix until just combined. Using a 2-ounce scoop, scoop the cookies onto a parchment-lined baking sheet, spacing them about 2 inches apart. Refrigerate overnight. (To freeze the cookie dough, place the baking sheet in the freezer for 1 hour, then transfer the cookie rounds to a resealable plastic bag and store in the freezer for up to 6 months.)

When ready to bake, preheat a convection oven to 375°F (or a regular oven to 400°F). Bake the cookies for 12 to 18 minutes, until the edges are golden brown. Let cool slightly before serving with a glass of ice cold milk.

Resources

The recipes in this book are, for the most part, flexible enough to be adapted to whatever ingredients are local and available to you. Starting your shopping at your local farmers' market is the best bet. But if you are running into roadblocks, there's a recourse. Luckily most things are now available for purchase online. Here are a few places to look.

PANTRY

Amontillado sherry
KL Wines
klwines.com

Banyuls vinegar
Zingerman's
zingermans.com

Barrel-aged maple syrup
Pappy & Co.
pappyco.com

Benne oil
Oliver Farm
oliverfarm.com

**Chiles de arbol,
chiles de pequin**
Kalustyan's
kalustyans.com

Chocolate
Videri Chocolate
viderichocolatefactory.com

Coarse sea salt
La Baleine
labaleine.com

Dijon mustard
Edmund Fallot
fallot.com

Dried field peas
Camellia Brand Lady Cream
peas or field peas
camelliabrand.com

Dried hibiscus
Mountain Rose Herbs
mountainroseherbs.com

Grits
Geechie Boy Mill
geechieboymill.com

Hot Sauce
Texas Pete Original Hot Sauce
texaspete.com

Olive oil
California Olive Ranch
Arbequina Extra Virgin
californiaoliveranch.com

Pedro Ximenez (PX) sherry
KL Wines
klwines.com

Piment d'espelette
Kalustyan's
kalustyans.com

Preserves and pickles
Farmer's Daughter
farmersdaughterbrand.com

Rice grits, Yellow Flint popcorn, Sea Island red peas, and benne seeds
Anson Mills
ansonmills.com

Fine sea salt
La Baleine
labaleine.com

Sorghum
Muddy Pond Sorghum
store.muddypondsorghum.net

Sultanas
Amazon.com
amazon.com

Tahini
Kalustyan's
kalustyans.com
I prefer Alwadi or Soom brand

Tellicherry peppercorn
Penzey's
penzeys.com

PRODUCE

These ingredients are usually available at our local farmers market when in season. I've noted the seasons to help you look for them at your own local markets.

Rose Finn Apple potatoes
Early to mid summer

Fresh field peas
Summer

Mustard frills
Spring, fall, and early winter

Green peanuts
Summer

MEAT, FISH, AND DAIRY

3-year aged cheddar
Hook's Cheese
hookscheese.com

Buttermilk
Cruze Farm
cruzefarm.com
I prefer Cruze brand from Tennessee, but any whole-fat buttermilk will do.

Fromage blanc
Murray's Cheese
murrayscheese.com

Whole duck, duck fat
D'artagnan
dartagnan.com

Country ham
Johnston County Hams
countrycuredhams.com

Whole octopus
Fresh Seafood
freshseafood.com
I can get fresh whole octopus from the seafood counter at Whole Foods, as well as my local seafood store; you can also order them frozen online.

EQUIPMENT

ISI whipper, Kitchenaid meat grinder attachment
Williams-Sonoma
williamssonoma.com

Sur La Table
surlatable.com

Pepper grinder
Unicorn Mills
unicornmills.com

Acknowledgments

Always remember there was nothing worth sharing, like the love that let us share our name.

—THE AVETT BROTHERS

To the Poole and Jordan families . . . Shirley and Leon, thank you for trusting me with your family name. It has truly been an honor to continue the legacy of this little diner that proved to be a very important piece of our great city. I promise we won't let you down.

To Robert "Fox" Christensen and Lynn Christensen, thank you for sharing with me the gardens and the bees, the flowers, and the importance of books and music. Thank you for the memories of the smell of food cooking in our home, and the joy of sharing. Thank you for opening my eyes and my heart to a love for entertaining—my greatest joy in life is found in sharing with others what you've shared with me. Thank you for this life.

To Eliza Kraft Olander, for believing in me, over and over again. You have made so many of my possibilities into realities. For all that you have taught me in the world of business, it's your generosity that inspires me the most. For all that I may achieve, you have shown me that the greatest reward exists in what I may do for others to help them recognize their potential.

To Kaitlyn Goalen . . . You signed on to manage my writing process, and you emerged as my co-author. This has been one of my favorite discoveries; all of my stories are better when you're a part of them. I remain in awe of your brilliance, both on the page and in everyday life. Thank you for your hard work, for believing in me, and for all of my flaws, loving me regardless. You are my best friend, and the light and love of my life. I'm so excited for our next chapter.

Thank you, David Black of the David Black Agency. You opened my mind to the value of our story, and you fought for my opportunity to tell it. You also hip-checked me on realistic timelines, and I'm so glad you did. I'll be a client as long as you'll have me.

To Jenny Wapner for being the first editor to reach out and ask if I'd ever considered writing a book. (I still remember turning to John T. Edge in the NYC cab we were sharing and saying, "Whoa! Someone wants to make a book with me!") As the concept became not so wild of an idea, you nurtured and developed my vision, and protected the integrity of my home, my story, and Poole's Diner. Together, I think we made something really special. Thank you for seeing the story in me before we ever met.

Thank you, Johnny Autry, for the incredible photographs that tell our story as much as our words.

Thank you, Charlotte Autry, for styling our shoots like you'd been with us since we opened the doors.

To Kara Plikaitis, Kate Bolen, Aaron Wehner, and the Ten Speed Press team . . . Thank you for all of your hard work on the backend that helped to turn a series of long headnotes into an actual cookbook!

To my brother, Zak Christensen . . . Remember when I was six years old and you told me that if I helped you take down the trash, we could form a special team, AND, you would let me name the team? I named us the Pac-Man Garbage Team. I was so proud as I dragged the bigger-than-me cans down the driveway in the cold, grinning ear to ear. You kind of pulled one over on me, but you taught me how much pride there is in being part of team, and how that pride can channel strength greater than we might physically embody at the moment. I've made a life of naming teams, and feeling a lot of pride. Teamwork makes the dream work. Thank you. I love you, bro.

And on the subject of brothers . . . Matt Kelly, I don't even know where to begin. You are both my favorite kitchen peer, and one of my greatest mentors. I look to you for guidance constantly. You are an incredible chef and one of the best pals a gal could dream up. Remember that time you wore your lucky Star Wars socks for me at the James Beard Awards? It worked DUDE! It worked!!! Proving yet again, you are a magical unicorn. I love you, pal.

To Team Poole's (our current team, and all members past) . . . YOU are my favorite piece of our story. It has been and continues to be a wild adventure, and I am honored to share it with each and all of you. I would do it all again, every single bit of it. "Work Hard, Play Hard."

To Matt Fern . . . Thank you for giving this place all you had in every moment. Together, we took Poole's to unimaginable places on one core ingredient . . . heart. Your beverage talents are boundless, but your role as head cheerleader has been my favorite. Clap your hands loudly, and continue making the world a better place.

Thank you Charlotte Coman for the incredible ground support through the production of this book. I needed someone who is as big of a freak for the details as I am, and with a love for this food as great as mine. My dear . . . you take the cake.

To Jason Tomaszewski . . . Your dedication to our food and your love for this little diner are immeasurable. I want you to know, Poole's loves you just as much as you love Poole's. Let's keep writing this story.

To Luke Buchanan . . . You have been with me since before Poole's Diner opened. You've worn so many hats (and hammers and paintbrushes), and you've never questioned giving each role a shot. You have on countless occasions been the man in my life. This place would not be the same without you, and neither would I. Thank you for the brilliant illustrations that helped bring this book to life, and thank you, for you. Life is rich and full . . .

To Andrew Ullom . . . In my lifetime, I have seen few people work as hard as you. The energy you bring to everything you touch in so inspiring. Your ability to approach every project uniquely and genuinely is a thing of beauty. You have built menus in all of our new places, and still honored our original path for Poole's. You've cut the sugar in half (against your better judgment) in desserts to appease salty me, and it's okay if you muttered under your breath while doing so (I would have too). You and Jess have made

Published in the United States by Ten Speed Press,
an imprint of the Crown Publishing Group,
a division of Penguin Random House LLC, New York.
www.crownpublishing.com
www.tenspeed.com

Ten Speed Press and the Ten Speed Press colophon are
registered trademarks of Penguin Random House LLC.

Library of Congress Cataloging-in-Publication Data
is on file with the publisher.

Hardcover ISBN: 978-1-60774-687-4
eBook ISBN: 978-1-60774-688-1

Printed in China

10 9 8 7 6 5 4 3 2 1

First Edition

Design by Kara Plikaitis
Lettering and illustrations by Luke Buchanan
Prop styling by Charlotte Autry

ASHLEY CHRISTENSEN is the chef and owner of seven restaurants—Poole's Diner, Beasley's Chicken + Honey, Fox Liquor Bar, Chuck's, Joule Coffee & Table, Death & Taxes, and Bridge Club—all located in downtown Raleigh, North Carolina. Ashley's cooking and her philosophy of bright, fresh flavors and locally grown, seasonal ingredients have garnered local and national acclaim. Ashley is involved in a number of charities, including the Frankie Lemmon Foundation, the Southern Foodways Alliance, and Share Our Strength. In 2014, Ashley was awarded the James Beard Award for Best Chef Southeast.

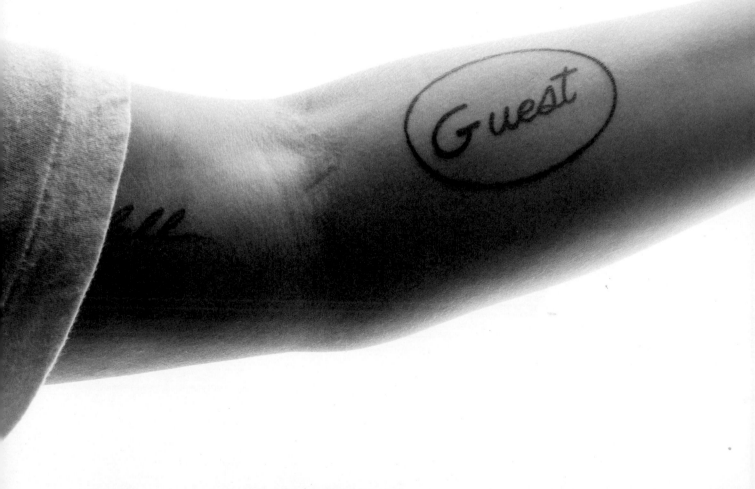